Pulse

Issue 2025-26

The Literary Magazine of Lamar University

Department of English and Modern Languages

Manufactured in the United States of America
ISBN: 978-1-962148-26-9

Dedication

This edition of *Pulse* is dedicated to the gifted and inspirational Dr. Amy Smith, in light of her recent publication, *Virginia Woolf's Mythic Method.*

Pulse Staff

Chief Student Editor
Claudia Cooper

Typesetter
Mikaela Bartlett

Poetry Editor
Mae Bradley

Prose Editor
Savanna Peveto-Kreatschman

Prose and Poetry Readers
Teri Wolfe, Britton Larson, Noah Carey, Mikaela Bartlett, Shakarral Singleton, Will Hammers, Brooke Groves, Jocelyn Rico

Cover Art: "Rose-Colored Lens" by Mae Bradley

Faculty Advisor
John Rutherford
Theresa Ener
Katherine Hoerth

Department Chair
Sara Hillin

Faculty Judges
John Rutherford
Damian Robles
Gretchen Johnson
Adam Nemmers
Kelsey Rall

Publication
Lamar University Press

Awards

Poetry — "Saint Valentine" by Mae Bradley

Poetry-in-Translation — "Ardiodeachas" by Mae Bradley

Creative Nonfiction — "A Knock at the Front Door" by Gillian Laird

Short Fiction — "Divided" by Jocelyn Rico

Scholarly Essay — "The Nature of *Hamlet*: Ecology in Ophelia's Death Scene" by Mae Bradley

Art — "Rose-Colored Lens" by Mae Bradley

Contents

Poetry

Poetry in Translation

Creative Nonfiction

Short Fiction

Scholarly Essays

Art

Alumni Spotlight

The Bloom is Off

Casey Ford

Thou, Sun, art half as happy as we ...
Shine here to us, and thou art everywhere;
This bed thy center is, these walls thy sphere.
—"The Sunne Rising," John Donne (1572-1631)

Stirred from bed, I'm lovely to you now.
My unabashed petals blush, arousing you;
the earth and perfume of my scent summon
you, who press your face into my folds
and praise the sun for its work in my grace,
knowing that our time is running out,
my beauty brief, your desire erratic,
choosing red one moment, blue the next

I begin to die from that first touch—
your brutal kiss has harmed me, cut me down
to so much less than what I might have been.
Though you will toss me out, I've value yet;
I'll feed the fertile ground with fruited heart.
May wiser fingers pluck the future out.

Asynchronous
Casey Ford

Any fool can know. The point is to understand. —Einstein

You sit in the snow of a thousand radios left on, voices overlapped in chat as a single, grey hum, center of the numb static, where you might remember what a radio even is. Mixed signals blur as rainwater on your eyelids. To learn is to reach out and tune the cold brass dial. The slow, deliberate turn, first feedback of a hundred clashing opinions, the dissonant noise of what you thought you knew. The zoom vibrates with grit, but your hand is steady. You are looking for the gap, the thin silence between frequencies, where the turmoil thins, mist lifting off a silver lake. A single note cuts through, not piercing, but it's got a pulse, and you know now, somehow, the noise was never the world, it was just the veil, and learning is the filter you build with your own tired, aching hands. You sing the note and finally hear yourself, not just another ghost in the wires, sole architect of the IP you inhabit. Hold the frequency tight until the music becomes your map.

Casey L. Ford (2013, 2015) is a proud graduate of the Lamar University Master of Arts in English program. She earned her MFA in Creative Writing from Fairfield University in 2022, and her first book of poems, *Shoreline Devotional*, is forthcoming from Woodhall Press this year. Casey is a mostly-lifelong resident of Southeast Texas, so her poems are often soggy with the sass and salt air of the region. She finds all poetry comes from looking at places where things intersect unexpectedly—gods and humans, wildflowers and roadkill, grief and a grocery aisle—and then articulating those intersections with all the beauty and harm words possess.

Poetry

Saint Valentine

Mae Bradley

The carnage glistens;
What follows a feast?
Pomegranate seeds smiling,
Dripping, juicy from your gums
And the smear of greasy, painted
Lips like plucking beaks
That probe in search
Of sanguine sweetness.
The bitten fruit
Supple and pink,
Cracked open for the breeze
That carries the lovebird's song.
The wiggling tongue,
Like a gust of wind
That thrusts itself upon
Vulnerable meat,
And flesh burned red
By the scooping-out and scraping
Of succulent pulp.
Knees that touch the ground
In prayer for
Divine offerings shared between
Two mouths at the altar,
Starving, still

Famished

Mae Bradley

I grew up hungry—
It's a cultural thing. You see,
Daddy's ribs were always showing.
It's family tradition.
We beg for work,
We make jack shit,
And then
the potatoes hit the table,
Just like always-
Except for when they didn't.
Except for when we went without.
Except for when we couldn't
Pay rent *and* eat.

When I was a little girl,
I fought for my meals.
It's family tradition.
My scarred forehead and
My sister's crooked jaw
Are proof that I'm no stranger
To fighting hand-to-hand.
We try to behave,
But little critters get scrappy
When the blight comes to take from us
What the British left behind.
Except for when we don't.
Except for when the food runs out.
Except for when the animals
are all too tired.

Even today, I follow the rules
Of the hungry working-man.
I clock out when my knuckles
Drip pink with bloodied sweat.
My debt burns low and slow
Like red-headed bodies
In a barren field. I check

"Caucasian" on applications,
But still get no response.

It's family tradition.
No Irish Need Apply.
Except for when I do.
Except for when I am qualified.
Except for when I start
My own tradition.

The Lovers by Dirac

Mae Bradley

I will never be loved like poetry.
The Mathematician sees
my body like a machine,
my brain like a computer,
my soul like a battery.

He peels me apart.
I'm laid out like a useless blueprint;
He assembles me by hand.
Raw materials,
Numbers and cuts—

He puts the pieces together,
The builder and the glue.
I love *him* like poetry.

He loves me like reality.

The Colonist

Mae Bradley

Companion poem for "The Architect," published in Pulse 2024-2025 edition

Now my lips are on the teacup
Instead of on the bottle
And the colonizer cracks his whip,
His horses run full-throttle.
Here he comes from far away
To conquer with his hands,
The god forsaken architect
With his castle made of sand.
And I thought for sure you'd never do
What was done to you before,
Even the most blessed man
Seems to only ask for more.
He who I praised like a god
Was really just a dog
Who raised his leg at things
He didn't even want.

I Don't Want Any Children

Jonas Hatch

I don't want any children.
I don't want them to be here,
In a world that is no fun,
Where no cheek is left without a tear.

For when they are born
I know black clouds will fly over head
And they will scrap for joy
'til the day they are dead.

I don't want any children.
It's a cruel fate indeed,
To plant into the dirt
An already withered seed.

For when they grow ill,
Who will wait beside their bed
To kiss them goodnight
As they shake and shiver; fever hot and red?

I don't want any children.
I couldn't bear to be around
And see in their eyes
No love to be found.

Will I be a good father
If my nightmares come to life?
Will I be able to provide them love and care;
Or a life full of pain and strife?

Ants

Jonas Hatch

There is that moment in our foundational years
Where we are trapped in our head daydreaming
More so than listening with our ears.
When eyes are open searching for each and every line
That cuts across the sidewalk like miniature roads
Carefully maneuvering our giant shoes—
Afraid to crush ant denizens that live below.

It is in our benevolence that we ponder,
    As we tip toe down the market square
Not a care in the world—no sonder—
        Looking up to see what we have always known:
            The bright blue skies and white fluffy clouds
                Beckoning us to play under their shade;
                    Only prone to anger on the saddest of days,
                        Yelling for us to come and play in the rain.

Though as we align our focus back to dodging cracks
Our eyes come to see something outside of our perfect existence.
A man or a woman dirtied and shrunken
With tattered clothes on their backs
Huddled under the shade of an alley or a business
Expecting to be thrown out like the wasteful food
                    That restaurants rid themselves of everyday
                    And to return alone once more without shelter.

At first, we are scared at this intrusion
To the utopia, that is our childhood.
Stepping away from them like they are a beast,
A stranger, a vagabond, a wolf that shall trick us
to dine with them in their cabin in the woods.
How can it be that one can live in misery
And yet still have some semblance of good remaining
in their hearts covered in the mud and refuse of poverty—
A concept that is foreign and unnatural to us.

Then they reach out to us as we pass by.
Their hands tainted with the dirt grasping
Before relinquishing with a sigh
and letting their arms slink back down as we pass
Never looking back trying to concentrate on our path,
Looking at the cracks dodging ants as we wonder
If we had just stepped on one.

A Morning Reflection at the State of My Surroudings

Jonas Hatch

Why do we brush the dust from our shelves
And paint the walls as they chip
Or fill the holes from which bugs and rodents creep
Into our homes—beneath our feet.

Why do we watch our weight and curse the scales
And walk the dogs as they yip and yell
Or brush our teeth as they rot away
And wake up only to rue the day
When our hands began to wither
And clothes began to fray.

Why should we control ourselves:
Fast at the break of day
Like the saints who hardly ever hear a prayer
Towards their own good name.

Why shan't we gorge ourselves
And let our bodies go to rot
For when day breaks we shall not care not.
For when the pain does reign
In our minds shall pleasure remain.

Why shan't we bury our homes in filth
As chaos and entropy shall take it over
As time comes to lay its claim
Upon our swollen bodies
As we rot where we did lay.

Why should we live constricting ourselves
Burying ourselves in our deeds
Laying down; building new seeds
Only for them to take upon them
The sins of their father.

Strawberry

Mikaela Bartlett

The summertime starts, yellow
berries on a basil-green bush.
It is warm outside, yellow
light infusing the air,
a tenderness. It is warm outside, and
I love you.

I want to taste the strawberries on your lips.

The summertime slows, lulling
a gentleness, a kindness.
It is warm inside, a blueberry-purple
pie bakes, cools, rests.
I love you, let's share a slice.

The summertime swirls, light
pink lemonade-bursts, a tingling
sweetness.
It is warm everywhere, I am warm
with you. I love you.

Let's picnic together.

The summertime sings, a spread
seafoam blanket ruffles, wings
awake in the easy wind.
A spread, tastefully earthy
and nutty and sweet, rich
dark wine, chocolate
strawberries, and
your lips.

I love you, let's eat strawberries together.

Great Appreciation for Big Dreams / No Respect for Little Plans

Mikaela Bartlett

You're smart, smarter than me, of course
you wouldn't take your coat.
It's summer, after all.
So of course, it hangs on the peg by the door,
in the corner of my eye, tricking me
into thinking you've just come home.
Of course, you haven't, I know what goodbye
tastes like. Your lips. Pomegranate, maybe.
The taste didn't linger long enough to tell.
Maybe you'll read this somewhere, some summer
where you're on a bus in Chicago, or New York,
or LA, or just Texas. You always had big dreams
and little plans. I was your little plan.
The coat's off the peg now. I wear it to bed and sweat.

Girlhood, Womanhood
Mikaela Bartlett

Be bold, be bold, they cry, and not
soft, never soft, you'll tear
and tear and tear up, drip drop,
down the cheek, to the floor,
under the feet. The feet stomp
and stomp. You're walking on glass,
crybaby. The ceiling's full of it.

Be soft, be soft, they whisper, and not
bold, never bold, you'll tear
and tear and tear through the glass, crash-smash,
on the floor, all over the floor, everywhere,
but especially under the feet. The feet stare
and stare. I'm kneeling at the feet.
My knees are full of glass.

Girl

Trinity Levins

I drove on little sleep
Hot water to wake up, eating with one hand on the wheel
It doesn't have to make sense
We stumbled into the field
Above the houses, the moon kept shining
For me, this is a lot more complicated,
But I think you are starting
to understand
I can only relax under a cover
A cover of dark, or smoke, or dark shiny liquid
A drain canal in a quiet neighborhood
I've never felt more understood
But to be you,
I could take up space
I could be anything
I don't know if you get what I mean
Invisible walls for me
You followed me up the stairs,
I followed you through the field
How do these things start?
There's nothing there, but then
there is.
I don't know how to write,
I think in pictures and give numbers colors
I feel like I'm coming apart and coming back together
I will never know you
And you will never know me
But we can try.

Hit

Trinity Levins

My hand is bruised in three places
from skating into a wall
It only hurts
when I am turning the wheel
I had wanted to keep up with my brothers
Their tall skinny frames and long curly hair
They know how to hug the curves and where to shift their weight
I had gone down the ramp
Gaining speed but lost balance
My legs hit the concrete,
and my hands gripped the rusty chainlink fence
Part of me wanted this,
Bruises up and down my arms and a bleeding finger
The same part of me that jumps in
knowing I will get thrown to the ground
The same part of me that dares my friend
to punch me in the face
The cuts and bruises prove I can withstand
I'm not strong, but I want you to know
I'm not weak
I have always been weak, a sore loser, an easy crier, sensitive, confused
If I'm not strong, I will make myself tough
I want to prove
that I can be a brother, too

Remember

Trinity Levins

I know we're not friends.
It's only summer, there's nothing better to do, and it seems
the hours we have to spend in your backyard
are endless.
Your eyes trace mine from the hammock to the dog
To the fence.
We can stay here in the gold and purple light at arms length.
This is how everyone is. His friends and his friends' friends and so on and so forth.
Listen, there's us and our people, and you and your people.
I do not know your name.
You don't seem to fit in this box.
You remembered that story I told you about my grandpa,
and how he died.
While everyone falls asleep, we crawl to the roof.
The sky is almost orange from the pollution, and I've spent
fourteen hours with you today.
We talk about video games, but really, your parents.
They don't know that.
It's like everyone makes a square, but I'm a circle and you're a star,
Really, I mean it.
Do other people ask you questions?
Does conversation make a friendship?
You say you don't know when to say no, but
I know you.
When drunk, you are more honest actually
I don't understand how you
go through life with bright eyes and four hours of sleep,
yet you always make time.
There's something you know about me, too.
It seems like we know this
but won't tell.
You are my best friend, I can't tell you that.
I like sitting in your passenger seat, I can't tell you that.
Instead, you will hug me when I leave and I will take note of when you pull away.

Instead, I will join you on the roof and you will say good morning.
We have nothing in common, except this.

Metamorphosis

Da'Vonna Martin

"Let us change you in the most sickeningly, beautiful
way possible," they introduced.
I stand behind with my hands folded
behind my back as I watch them mush and
bind this sculpture.

It moves like its flesh.
my eyes glides from its feet to its head.
I reach its gaze, is this flesh?
It stares back at me intensely.
"Get a feel of it, why don't you?" they murmur
in unison around me.

I stay still and I watch. Its gaze continues
to stare at me but this time with hatred,
with dissatisfaction, desperation.

I can't move. My eyes don't leave its own. its
lips start moving. Almost with a sense
of familiarity, its teeth grits with frustration.
Its eyes brimming red, low with sorrow.
"I am not satisfied."

I look around me and nothing changes.
They're still carving and shaping.
every sweep and pull of their wretched hands
manipulates this sculpture.
No way can this be a sculpture.

"it's not your art anymore, it's ours. You stand
there and let us make our art." They chatter.
i watch as its body vibrates with sorrow.
its lips move, "stop! get your hands off."
you're not supposed to touch art, right?'

my lips move but my words rest unheard. I
look down from this pedestal.

to these people surrounding me, touching
me, morphing me into the art they deem fit.

"Pure and utter perfection that is. Artistic
stomach is what we would call it."
They began standing back
one by one. hands locked behind their back.

A Simpler Time

Bronwyn Jones

golden rays filter through fresh dewdrops that quiver
with the low coo of mourning doves and effervescence of cicadas,
tucked somewhere under the shady fig tree.

my window cries with the rising sun, tears falling in harmony
with the shedding of a new day. i pick a drop and follow it,
hoping it wins the imaginary race in my head.

a lone dragonfly lands on a bush of baby's-breath.
i study its iridescence, blue-green magic that i see
in my own eyes. perched so still on a puff of white perfume.

the backyard is a sandbox of memories and upturned
rocks from a day of play, writhing with roly-polies
and worms that yearn for the coolness of wet clay and shade.

On Getting a Taste of Accessible Transportation and Third Spaces

Jeri Wolfe

Yearning since my global travels
To taste a little taste
Of life outside of elderly cars with odd squeaks,
To nibble on bicycle pedals
And relish the richness of gourmet bike lanes.
A decadent scent of footsteps on paved, not cracked, sidewalks
floats me to small cafés and storefronts
where outside bricks easily meet the inside tile.
The flavor of gasoline is bitter when landing on a
Softer, cleaner palate.

This is an acquired taste, I presume,
As being served porcelain plates in a Spanish brunch spot
brings out the lip-smacking taste of homemade pastimes.
The stark tang of sour Styrofoam to-go boxes and plastic cups
Creates a new craving of mine own.
This hunger—an urgent need—
Slices through my Sysco-fed loaf of life,
Teasing my appetite with the tiniest crumbs of
a nutrient-rich diet of sunshine, movement,
and a gourmand world free to roam.

For what it's worth,
I will choose to eat my old meals,
Even if my days are less grand in zest.
To sustain my life with what is given
Provides an insight on meals that differ,
And I can still relish the thoughts with savor.

Golden Shovel State

Hailey Waobikeze

Cold streets hum, I'm numb but awake,
Dreams cut deep, every move's high-stake.
Cool on the surface, heat in the chest plate,
Time don't wait, it just dictates fate.

Seven shadows posted, chalk on the curb,
Skipped that class, learned code from the word.
Slide through smoke, where the rules get blurred,
Talk slick quick, every line inferred.

Grind till the lights fade, dice hit cement,
Hope in a flask, broke but intent.
Sin for the win, thin gin for the scent,
Every prayer half-said, half-spent, repent.

Cold streets hum, I'm numb but awake,
Dreams cut deep, every move's high-stake.
Cool on the surface, heat in the chest plate,
Time don't wait, it just dictates fate.

No sleep, 'cause rest gets taxed,
Mind on defense, soul still maxed.
Cool kids front, but the fear's beneath,
Where a grin hides pain, and the gain's too brief.

Ink drip real, I bleed what I write,
City don't care who prays at night.
We too slick, too smart, too soon,
Cool in the heat, still hum that tune.

Cold streets hum, I'm numb but awake,
Dreams cut deep, every move's high-stake.
Cool on the surface, heat in the chest plate,
Time don't wait, it just dictates fate.

The poem "Golden Shovel State," written by Hailey Waobikeze, combines the spirit of Gwendolyn Brooks's "We Real Cool" and Nas's "N.Y. State of Mind." It shows how pride and survival exist side by side in the lives of young people growing up in dangerous environments. Waobikeze uses rhythm, imagery, and repetition to express how confidence can also hide fear, and how time and fate shape people's lives in the city.

The form of the poem follows a rap style, using short lines and strong rhymes to create a steady beat. The repeated hook, "Cold streets hum, I'm numb but awake, / Dreams cut deep, every move's high-stake," works like a chorus in a song and reminds the reader that the speaker lives in a constant state of alertness. This repetition reflects Brooks's use of recurring "we" phrases in We Real Cool. Both techniques build rhythm while showing how the speaker's world repeats the same patterns of risk and struggle. The rhyme and flow are also influenced by Nas's storytelling style, which captures the fast, dangerous pace of street life.

The speaker of the poem represents both an individual and a group. He speaks for himself, but he also reflects the shared experience of those living in the same conditions. The line "Seven shadows posted, chalk on the curb" alludes to Brooks's seven pool players and connects their sense of rebellion to the modern street setting. The speaker has pride, but that pride is mixed with fear. He knows his "cool" is not only about appearance but survival. When he says, "Grind till the lights fade, dice hit cement," the line shows how his world is ruled by risk and chance. Every decision feels urgent, and even small choices can have heavy consequences.

The poem's central message focuses on time and how it controls life. The line "Time don't wait, it just dictates fate" carries the same sense of mortality that Brooks suggests when she writes, "We die soon." In both cases, time is an unstoppable force. The characters in these works live with the awareness that their lives could end at any moment. Still, the poem also shows persistence and strength in facing that truth.

Emotionally, the poem mixes confidence with sadness. The rhythm and rhyme show energy and determination, but the imagery suggests loss and exhaustion. Lines like "Hope in a flask, broke but intent" describe people who hold on to faith even when their situation is difficult. The poem's musical tone makes the message easier to feel.

Through its form, sound, and voice, "Golden Shovel State" honors Brooks's rhythm and Nas's detailed realism. It captures how young people try to stay "cool" and in control while living in an environment that constantly challenges them. The poem's power comes from showing both their pride and their pain.

2:51am

Oakley Eligio

I am friends with the dark,
With the beings that hide inside
I have danced with the late night shadows
Laughed with the monsters under my bed

Because it is only when the hour grows late
And the sleeping world shrinks to fit behind my curtains
That time and reality fall away and I am free

And so I drift,
Spinning through the void
Cocooned in my conscious
The only person alive

(But then there is you
Hushed giggles
And bad audio quality

A person held aloft
By the thin strings of my mind
And a 5 by 2 fluorescent screen

We are something cradled in the stars
Born in the space between your brain and voice
I reach for you in the void

And you aren't real

Neither of us are

But maybe, just maybe
I can find myself in your warm laughter
And you can find yourself in my slurred words
And maybe we could know each other

In the quiet space of 2:51 am)

Cavernous is the Girl I Met

Teri Wolfe

Through the crumbling labyrinth
of her open mouth,
I hope to catch a glimpse of the
girl within.
Like a pickaxe to stone,

I chip my way through her stone
walls

that blocks my view.

In reality, I don't know her.
I only recognize the way she smiles

politely when she listens to
whatever mud spills from my
tongue, raw and authentic. I wear

my hands dirty for her to see

I am not here to steal anything.

When she speaks, she doesn't
spew dirt.

She tells me the value of her riches
as gold crumbles from the gaps in
her teeth.
The words are brittle and brassy,

impersonating the softness of the
real thing.

She is full of fantasy
a California rush.

She talks about glistening
men in denim

with respect that
charms her
and arms that hold her,
and she swallows these ideas
of who they
really are.
To me, these men are
covered in soot.

They mine for coal in hopes
of gold.
They will never see the girl
beyond appearance, beyond
the flashy reflection on her
surface. I warn her, and

she knows this—still, she
suffocates on unrealistic
love with diamond eyes.

Does she know who she is,
beyond being the fool?
Does the inside crave what
the outside shows?

As she sips from her margarita,
the gold flakes into her drink
and the image of cocktail dresses
and wine sipping makes its way in.

In between the stalagmites
and stalactites guarding her
mouth, I hope she knows
she can crawl out.

Thoughts While Doing My Own Laundry

Teri Wolfe

Like an ugly red blotch on my favorite shirt,
men are permanent in my life.
They are soaked into the linen I wear
and how I wear it.

I hate how I've allowed them to seep
into the darkest color fabric,

making their presence always known.
I could wear the thinnest crop top

or the heaviest sweater,
and they will bleed through

and discolor my own flesh.

I've been told

to use soap made by them,

and I'm expected to clean
the messes they make, too.
And I try—
but how can I wash these blemishes out
when they've forcefully dyed
the center of my being?

Maybe I should to clean it at all.
I could throw away the jeans they've ripped open,

I could wear less
to keep my clothes from getting tainted,

I could wear more

to keep myself from getting filthy.

Yet I am told it is my fault that
all my whites have turned pink.

As I take my laundry out the dryer
and fold my defiled clothes,
I ask:
Is it really up to me alone

to scrub the stains out

with my own bare hands?

Following is a collection of poems written by William Hammers, entitled "Emotions Never Spoken," with themes of masking, unrequited, impossible, or forbidden love, isolation, morality, and LGBTQ+.

Contents

Acting

I shiver inside and these tears I do hide
From those who might actually care

My fear is so cold, yet my anger is bold
Why can't these burdens I share

These words that I write do tell of the fight
Which I veil from the rest of the world

That thin little line, which I pace in my mind
Between calm and emotions unfurled

I'm certainly no stranger to my fear and my anger
So why do I disguise them, I ask

Why do I lie and try to deny
My feelings behind this mask

I put on this act, until it's almost a fact
But the curtain is coming down

And those tears which I hide are starting to slide
As my personal play comes unbound

Lifeline

Each and every endless day, the same old shade of unfeeling gray

Day in day out, the same routine, a lonely cog in this endless machine

I yearn each day for your fiery embrace, a blazing pyre that helps keep my pace

But the flame we fanned is burning out, until your love I begin to doubt

I cry out to you from this uncaring heap, because of that spark which you alone keep

The darkness your fire once kept at bay, slowly creeps in as your comfort fades away

With no warmth left to call my own, the cold begins to freeze my bones

I'm spiraling downward, falling within, the embers of your love a lifeline so thin

But grasp it I must until my work is through, because the only thing keeping me alive is you

Blind

My eyesight begins to grow ever dim
As I think of you with him

Colors begin to bleach to gray
I hate that my love won't just fade away

Shapes before me begin to blur
Why did I believe our devotion was so sure

That fading gray, finally, bleeds to black
And it kills me that I still want you back

But as my world goes dark for the final time
I'll let you go for, you'll never be mine

The Apple

I first loved you in that Garden of Eden
Amongst our friends laughing, playing, and singing

Taught the feeling was wrong, that it could never last
I locked my love inside, hoping that emotion would pass

But like the Apple of Knowledge, I still had that bite
Finding out that love wouldn't just fade without fight

Eve offered Adam just one little taste
Which ruined them both and brought them disgrace

Could I do the same and ruin your fate
I wonder inside, I wonder and wait

Time Tickles Me

Isabella Deese

Time tickles me on the stained plaid couch.

Persistent.

I filled the metal canoe up with water/
hot summer days, splashing my brother.
                                        Plunging forward into brown, green, blue, sea
        down
            down, to the color of skeletons chattering in the sand.
            still in line while i run;
I run more empty Golden espresso
Shots. Firing out drink after drink to the pumpkin heads,
rolling from the Gulf, to the marshes, to the plains, to my front yard.
Sitting here Oil leaked from that ancient white ford,
chalk outlined on green grass turned upside down
        In the fishbowl of strawberry mint soap.

Bubbles to End the World

Isabella Deese

Crack open the world
Can of soda
pop
          pop
pop
Cold summer day

Stars enter invade my
      veins. Smoke fills my nose
s'mores and strawberries in
   my throat Sticking to
vocal cords to trachea to esophagus to
pop   *pop*
   pop   *pop*
pop *pop*

Be Silent

Isabella Deese

Sometimes I think about us.
I wish I wouldn't
I wish couldn't

It bubbles in my throat
stiches threating to
B u r sT
A tornado's cry

Silence

And you,
floating past me
Hands trembling
Eyes on the floor
a smile

I wonder
what I would say if
I was
brave enough

After Removing My Wisdom Teeth, I Had A Really Weird Dream Where My Gums Kept Swelling Up And Falling Out

Claudia Cooper

but there was no blood. Thank God.
I just could not talk.

My gums were flesh-jelly, made of inflamed pulp and pulsating ice.
My tongue trapped between bloated tissue tumbled
to make muffled sounds from a mouthful of crimson marshmallows.

Like a sick toddler, I spat out
chewed-up copper-flavored bubblegum in my hands.
Each time my panicked lips parted
I puked more pink pap in my palms.

Then, I woke up
and realized the backward tilt of my head,
coaxing my cotton-crammed mouth open,
vulnerable.

Daycare

Claudia Cooper

Colors flashed everywhere:
celery green walls, evergreen carpet,
white linoleum speckled with gold flakes.
A red T-rex bit into the neck of an orange Triceratops.
A yellow caterpillar crawled away from a grey spider.
The pink plastic doll house
with the baby blue roof and ivory floors
stood tall in the center.
Pale Barbies with frizzy blonde hair
or tangled brunette hair or shiny red hair
filled the space.
The space I filled was small.
Tucked away in a dark cubby,
a black-and-white alien soldier
like me, assessed the carpeted terrain,
watching over the human race.
Today, no one looked like me.
Tan, beige, splotchy red, white.
I was the only Brown.

Ideals

Rylee Zapotoschny

Opening the chest door dims the sting of golden lamp light.

The parting of its contained force
corrupts the weightless air.

Closing the door now leaves its contents
painfully distinguished—

creaking from many operations,
dull, brash hardware
idolized in the presence of another time.

Viewing the contents, now reeking with questions,

the night reveals what remains
a starvation of visions
still shaped like inherited dreams

recognized without knowing *why*

Guatemalan Coffee

Alexander Lara

guatemalan beans

we were planted in the country they destroyed,
for we did not align with their rules.

we are grown by watchful eyes; we all stay in place.
the beans must be harvested for their enjoyment.

we are pushed through a ripping grinder to be made small,
packed with others they believe are the same.

our packaging we are stored in, shows art that was stolen.
changed to be more aesthetic in their standards.

collecting us like prizes for their homes
concerned only with our appearance.

stowed in the cold to not lose flavor,
kept in the dark until we needed, was this our fate?

irresistible at the start,
yet if not enjoyed, we are replaced by another.

H2O2

Lucas Infante

Off putting hours will not save you from
Your heart's ache, nor will it rid you of their spread

Grievances of "not enough days"
You shout, yet you remain stagnant in your endeavors

Regardless of age, it will rot if left untouched
Get a move on before the spores postulate

Open the window and spritz a little H_2O_2
If not, you too will rot

Not from it, but from within it
All by your own fungal infested hands

Return to Sender

Lucas Infante

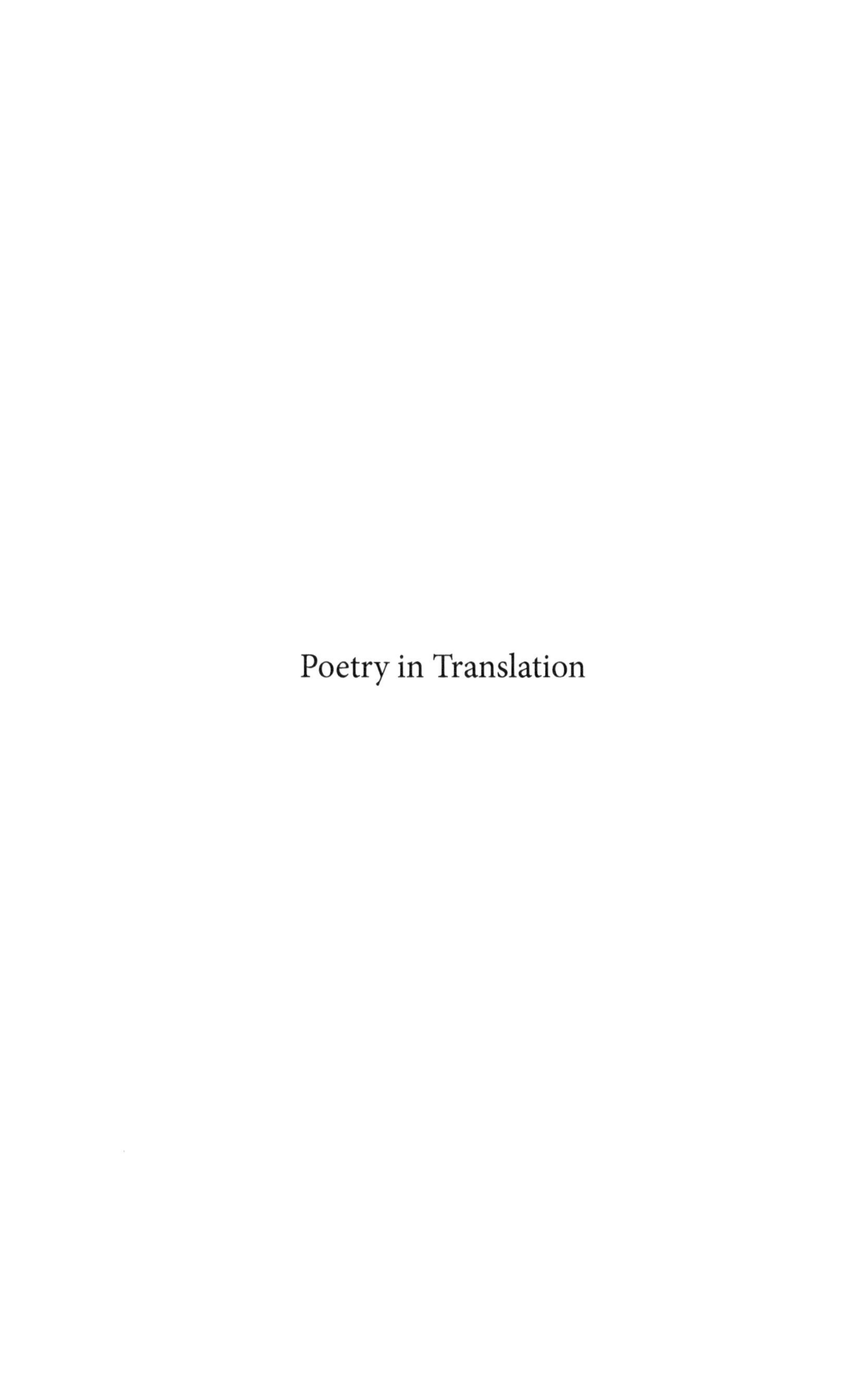

Poetry in Translation

Ardiodeachas

Mae Bradley

Páiste ar scoil,
Múinteoir agus dalta,
Gach ceann níos cliste
Ná an chéad cheann eile.
Gach lá a chuardaím
Na focail ceart
Ach tá I gcónai
Níos mó le foghlaim.
Mar atá sa scoil
Mar sin atá an saol;
An foclóir atá á léamh agam fós.

Higher Education

A child in school,
Teacher and student,
Each smarter
Than the next one.
Every day I search for
The right words
But there are always
More to learn.
As in the school
So is life;
The dictionary I am still reading.

Writer's Note

This poem is my own original work, initially written in Irish and translated to English for reader convenience. I thought writing about my failure to communicate growing up as a multilingual child in a monolingual household was a task best executed in my third language, offering me a challenge during the writing process that mirrored those I faced during my upbringing.

Translation of Rhyme X by Gustavo Adolfo Becquer

Adithleidy Lopez-Magallon

Rima X

Los invisibles átomos del aire
en derredor palpitan y se inflaman,
el cielo se deshace en rayos de oro,
la tierra se estremece alborozada.

Oigo flotando en olas de armonías,
rumor de besos y batir de alas;
mis párpados se cierran... ?¿Qué sucede?
¿Dime?
¡Silencio! ¡Es el amor que pasa!

Rhyme X

The invisible atoms of the air
around palpitate and inflame,
the sky comes undone in rays of gold,
the earth shudders exhultantly.

I hear floating waves of harmony,
rumors of kisses and flapping of wings;
my eyelids close....? What is happening?
Tell me?
Silence! It is the love that passes by!

Hijo

Alexander Lara

hijo

aunque tus ojos no han abierto,

te he robado de esta vida.
por la justicia no ha llegado

dentro mi corazon.

¿soy un criminal?

aunque nunca te he visto,
mis deseos ya te conocen.

que la sangre que me he dado vida,

un dia llegara en ti.

por cuato yo te amo,
te rechazo este regalo
pero cuando me veo al espejo,
nuestros reflejos de la misma
imagen.

mi hijo, daniel alexander

son

though your eyes
have yet to open,
i have robbed you of this life.
for justice has yet to be
delivered
within my heart.

am i a criminal?

though i have never seen you,
my dreams have already met
you.
that the blood that has given
me life
will one day flow through you.

because i love you,
i deny you this gift.
but as i look in the mirror,
our reflections display the
same image.

my son, daniel alexander

Creative Nonfiction

A Knock at the Front Door

Gillian Laird

Most parents teach their children things like how to ride a bike, how to tie their shoes, how to not be an asshole. Mine taught me to never open the front door. There I sat, just two years old, on the living room floor of my home—a weathered, white hovel in the bad part of town—playing with my dollar store toys and bothering the family cat. My mother had left for class a few hours before, and my father had just gotten into the shower. When I heard a knock at the door, I did what I had seen them do countless times. I got up and answered it.

Towering over me stood a man with close-cropped hair and a tattered orange shirt. To me he looked like a silly cartoon character from the shows I'd watch on a Saturday morning. To him I was a nuisance he didn't anticipate. "Hi—uh—are your parents home?" He asked.

"Yeah, my daddy's in the shower," I responded. "I'll go get him."

Waddling through the living room and down the hall, I did exactly that. I opened the unlocked bathroom door and rushed into a wall of steam. Over the hum of the water, I said, "Daddy, there's a man at the door." My father didn't seem to mind much until I looked over my shoulder, caught sight of a shadow and said, "He's waiting for you in the living room."

Without wasting a second, my father threw back the shower curtain, naked as the day he was born, grabbed a towel to wrap around his waist and barreled into the hallway, pushing me behind his hulking figure. "What the hell are you doing, man?" His voice boomed.

Eyes bulging, the intruder, intimidated by the sheer size and muscle of my father (he liked to body-build in his spare time), didn't waste a second in bolting for the door and fleeing out onto the street. I watched as my father followed him, fists clenched at his sides. But instead of chasing him out like he really looked like he wanted to, he simply shut the door and locked it tight. I felt like I was flying when he then scooped me up into his arms and took me into my bedroom.

There, he set me down on the rough carpet and stared down at me, shower water still running in the distance, rivulets pouring down his body. "Why did you do that, Gillian?" He asked me. When he called me by my name, I knew I was in trouble.

It was always Gills, Gillie, Gill, or Skeen (don't ask). But never Gillian. My full first name was reserved for a good telling-off.

Looking all over at my light purple walls, at my crib, at the bookcase against the wall and the pacifier on the second shelf from the bottom, I stated the obvious, unable to quell my sarcasm, even at two: "You and Mommy do it."

"I know, but you can't ever do that again," he said, pointing a finger at me. I suppose it was meant to be menacing.

But I still asked: "Why?"

"Because that man was a stranger. He could have..." He trailed off, clearly perturbed at having to explain something to a two year old that I likely wouldn't even understand.

But I did.

"He could have taken you away or stolen our things, or he could have hurt you," my father finally blurted. "Don't ever open the front door again."

I nodded, watching as the sticky stars and crescent moon stuck to the ceiling seemed to lose some of their glow. In that moment, all I could do was lock my father's words—his warning—into my mind, and it wasn't until I grew older that I dared to wonder why I was left alone at two years old in the first place. But that's what happens when your entire existence stems from an accident made by two nineteen-year-old kids. In another life I would have been a statistic in an abortion pamphlet, but my mother believed that it was God's will for two children to have a child. As far as my father was concerned, he loved my mother and that was enough. So into this world I came, black-haired and squinty-eyed.

It wasn't long after the fated Front Door Debacle that my family and I moved into a new house in a safer area. My parents both had good jobs and were working their way up in the world, my mother as an ultrasound tech and my father as a police officer. By seven years old, I had a baby brother. Mom and Dad tried hard for him. His bedroom was directly across the hall from mine.

During the day, my bedroom looked like any little girl's dream.

Two walls were pink and two were yellow, and a Barbie Dream House stood in the corner. Rows of stuffed animals and American Girl dolls sat on the fluffy, white carpet on one side of the queen-sized bed. This was where I liked to read to my toys, pretending I was a teacher or a mother.

Everything felt different at night.

I had a TV stationed across from my bed, surrounded by Disney VHS tapes and CD's burned with movies pirated by my grandfather. They never worked, always freezing a few minutes in as if the disc was scratched. Spending twenty minutes rewinding my Barbie of Swan Lake VHS seemed like a better way to waste my time on the nights my dad worked late. My mother had long since grown too busy with her other children to spend much time with me. But I didn't mind. Being the most mature seven year old of all time, I understood. Besides, I had my dolls and my movies and my books to keep me company while I waited up for my dad. Though I'd always fall asleep well before he even left the station.

One night, my eyes grew heavier than usual, and I could no longer deny the pull of sleep. So I pushed back my floral comforter, tugged my stuffed puppy close, and drifted off. It felt like only seconds before I woke again to a dark, silent house. Laying there in the shadows I found myself staring across the hall towards my brother's room, my eyes struggling to adjust to the darkness. My dad liked us all to keep our doors open at night. Something about the air conditioner running better that way, he said. I remember thinking that was ridiculous as I blinked to clear the grain from my vision. Suddenly, something like a ghostly figure manifested in my brother's doorway.

Short and hooded like the Grim Reaper from The Grim Adventures of Billy and Mandy—the only thing I had to compare the ghostly figure to—it suddenly started to move. Closer and closer it drifted as I waited to feel its frosted claws rip me from my bed, taking me away to some dark corner of the world where my mommy and daddy would never find me, just like my dad had warned me. I yearned to be able to slam the door on it like I had seen my father do all those years ago, but I felt glued to my mattress.

So I did the next best thing: I hid under the blankets. I kept telling myself it was only my imagination, though it felt horrifyingly real to my young mind. Even now, as an adult, I still sometimes wonder whether or not it was.

It didn't feel like I could come up for air again until, when I was eleven, my family expanded thanks to the arrival of another little brother and we moved houses. Again. This one was big and made of brick and in the safest part of town. My dad had been promoted twice, and my mom got a raise at the cardiology office. My little brothers wouldn't have to share a room now.

One evening during my freshman year of high school, I found out that I made the school dance team. I remember rushing to the result sheet that was posted at the front of the school, friends in tow.

I remember how we all took photos together in front of it, pointing at our names and making kissy faces for the camera. I remember the girls who didn't make it, crying in the background. I remember going home, where I sat on my new purple and blue comforter, my parents on either side of me and a box of old photographs in front of us.

"This is from my first football game," my mom said as she pulled out a crinkled photo, August 1997 dated on the back. In the photo, my mom beamed at the camera with her friends, all of them donning tiny red skirts, white boots, and sequin tops with a big, white star in the middle. Pom-poms in hand and a cowgirl hat on their heads, they looked like the poster children for small-town America.

I never said it out loud, but I deeply wished to be given the exact same uniform my mom wore so more people would have the excuse to keep telling us how much we looked alike. But it wasn't true. She's always been prettier than me. She's always been more admired than me, with her dark hair and her freckles and her high cheekbones, her tan skin and her waist that's shaped like a Disney Princess's.

"And this was our senior prom," my mom said as she pulled out another photo. In it, my parents stood together, grinning from ear to ear. My mom wore a black satin dress, her hair piled on her head, while my father wore a suit that starkly contrasted the bleached tips of his hair and the earrings sparkling in his ears. "The passenger seat was broken in your dad's truck, so when he picked me up I had to sit in the backseat."

I looked to my father, his balding head outlined by the boyband posters on the wall behind him. "Grandma didn't let you drive her car?" I asked incredulously.

"Not a chance," Dad laughed, the smile on his face matching the one in the photo.

As the night wore on, I gathered a small collection of photos from my parents' high school experience, pinning them on my bulletin board amongst a smorgasbord of other memories, like concert tickets and wristbands, polaroids and middle school achievements. Taking a step back, I stared at the new additions to the board, secretly hoping that some of my parents' memories would manifest into my own.

Only a few weeks into the following school year, an older boy messaged me on social media. I'll call him Jonathan.

Jonathan talked to me all the time, but when we saw each other in the halls he acted like I didn't exist. I didn't mind. My face went as red as a cherry every time I spotted his curly hair in the crowd of students traveling at a snail's pace to get to class, so the odds of me actually being able to speak back were pretty slim.

"I'm in love!" I would eventually say—but not about Jonathan or any of the other boys in my classes. No, I was in love with each new bit of fan memorabilia I added to my bookshelves, to my walls, my personal effects six feet below it all. Because in my mind, unlike Jonathan—who things didn't work out with—the celebrity men that I romanticized would have actually spoken to me in the halls. And in my head, if they would have knocked on the door, whether my parents were home or not, I would have thrown it open and spoken back.

Eventually high school screeched to a stop, and I couldn't stand my room. I couldn't stand my life. Crowded with Pop-Funkos, posters of British celebrities, books I hadn't read, and photos with people I wasn't friends with anymore, my bedroom felt a lot like my brain. Overused. I couldn't wait for a break from it all. I just never imagined that break would come in the form of a worldwide pandemic dragging the world by its hair to a halt.

"How long do you think this will last?" I asked my best friend at the time, Maya.

Together we sat on the hood of my Volkswagen, staring out at the small pond of water before us. We were parked in the grass, a spring breeze whistling through the blades and tickling the wildflowers. Everything was so quiet. The world had gone silent—and I liked it. But I could never admit that. How are you supposed to proudly admit that you're happy the rest of the world is as scared to open their front door as you are? People were hurting. They were dying. And I was drowning in graduation money that I spent as fast as I got it on things like coffee and One Direction merchandise from Etsy, because people felt bad I wasn't getting a prom.

"Not long, I hope," Maya responded as the sun disappeared behind the clouds.

"Yeah. Me too."

Seven months later, I started college and got my first job. Wearing pink masks and pastel yellow shirts, hair pulled back, I spent my days serving coffee and pastries to the women in my town who could afford an $8 chocolate chip cookie.

As the days bled into months and masks and crinkled eyes were exchanged for unhidden smiles, the pandemic phased out. From all the time spent in my car, I had pearls hanging from my rearview mirror, scrunchies lining the gearshift, a garland of fake flowers strewn across the dashboard, and 97,000 miles on it. I numbly watched that number continue to grow as I drove to work on a Wednesday afternoon.

"Gill," my boss said over FaceTime thirty minutes after I tied my apron around my neck and sat at the register for yet another shift of staring out the windows and listening to the same Taylor Swift songs on loop. Boss lady's—I'll call her Ursula, since she had an odd obsession with her underage employees and letting us all know she could sing—moon-shaped face took up most of the screen as she drove, eyes glued to the phone instead of the road the entire time. "Did you accept a $100 dollar bill at any point this week?"

"No, I don't think so. I think I'd remember if I did," I responded, half-listening to Ursula and half-listening to my fellow employees giggle as they got rowdy in the back, leaving me to do all the work by myself up front, per usual.

"Well someone did, and they didn't use the pen to check if it's a fake. Look." Ursula dropped the phone as she reached for the bill. Watching as she finally put it in front of the camera, all I could see was what looked like the black marking of a sharpie through Benjamin Franklin's face. "It's not real, and I need to know which one of you did it. I'll check the cameras."

Ursula liked to watch her employees on the cameras stationed around her business like it was a Kardashian's marathon. She loved to remind us that she did this too, always saying she could hear everything we said about her and each other. I so badly wanted to tell her that was bullshit. At home, we had security cameras outside and in our house. My dad has a thing about safety. But I knew they didn't have sound, and they sure as hell wouldn't produce a suspect. Not with that grainy footage.

Nonetheless, I passed the phone to each employee on shift that day like Ursula commanded, and each of them denied ever having seen the supposedly fraudulent $100 bill. Eventually, the boss showed up at the shop, stomping in wearing her Dr. Martens and leggings, her footsteps echoing along the linoleum floor as she marched up to the register. She waved the worn bill around, flashing it in front of all of our faces, as if to prove it was real. "I tried to take it to the bank, and they wouldn't accept it."

"I thought you went to get your nails done," one of my co workers murmured.

"And then I went to the bank, duh," Ursula said, waving around the $100 with nails that looked like it taken the tech at least two hours to finish—which was exactly how long she'd been gone.

As I watched Ursula continue to bombard each individual who worked for her about the hundred-dollar bill that looked a little too real to be as fake as she claimed, I daydreamed about going home and kicking my feet up in my room. I'd probably light the pink, rose scented candle on my bedside table, turn on the fairy lights above my bed, and put a vinyl on the record player in the corner. I'd stare at the newly empty wall to the left of my bed, recalling how I tore down each and every poster in a rage the week before, because the celebrities in them would care only about me as much as the everyman cared about their paycheck. I'd wonder what to fill the space with. Then I'd pull a book from the two-foot stack of unread books by my door and disappear, hiding from the workplace worries that followed me into every facet of my life.

Eventually Ursula grew tired of receiving the same answers: no one had seen the bill before. So she handed it to the dish boy and said, "Go spend this at the deli next door. I'm hungry for lunch."

If my dad couldn't jump out of the shower and scare Ursula out of my house, I'd have to leave myself. So I threw my apron off and walked out the front door without looking back.

At twenty-three, I moved to a new apartment, in a new city. My mom's tears still drenched my sweater from when we said goodbye earlier that day. As I walked up the stairs, avoiding a set of busy elevators, I held the last of the boxes in my arms. It overflowed with stuffed animals and books and posters and pictures and old records, all stuff that would likely stay in that very box, collecting dust at the top of my new closet.

Pulling the key from my pocket, I unlocked the front door, stepped inside, and locked it again. I placed the box on the gray marble of the kitchen counter and then flicked on the overbearing fluorescent lights. Looking around at the white walls, the slate floor, and the windows that showed a foreign city, I realized how unready I actually felt. So I took the box off the counter and walked into the bedroom—a room just as empty as the rest of the apartment.

Forgoing the light switch, I sat in the center of the floor and began pulling the tape off the box. One by one, I pulled each childhood memento out and set them in a circle around me. The only light I could see by was the hazy, navy glow of the city life outside.

Blindly untangling the fairy lights, I felt along the wall for an outlet and plugged them in. They still worked. With a better view of the trinkets and memories around me, I filtered through them all. Finding a blue scrunchie from my sophomore year of high school, I slipped it on my wrist. Then I found a gold heart locket that I bought myself at nineteen, pretending a boyfriend had given it to me, and clasped it around my neck. I had long since ripped the picture out of it. Reaching for a stuffed pink and white dog, I remembered how I begged my grandma to buy me a bedazzled dog leash that I would attach to it for walks around the house when I was six. Bringing it to my nose, the roughened fur smelled like mildew and happiness. I found an old work shirt from my first job, one that I forgot to throw out with the rest.

Then I found a polaroid of Maya and I outside a concert venue, proudly showing off our middle fingers because the concert had been canceled due to a hurricane that never even touched down. I found a photo of my old co-workers and I from when we were still friends, and I found one of me hugging my little brothers close. I found a crumpled up poster of an English singer I really used to like and I found a special edition magazine for a movie franchise that used to make me smile. I found a broken strand of pearls and a petal-less garland of fake flowers. I found receipts and pamphlets and paper wristbands.

I found my polaroid camera.

With it in hand, I walked to the corner of my new room, and I snapped a photo of it, naked and new. It was done developing by the time I reloaded the box with all of my childhood things. And it was then that someone knocked on the door. The sound echoed off the empty walls, bounced off the gray ceiling and fake wooden floors. Just as I had been as a child, there I was, sitting on the floor and playing with my toys. Playing with my memories. For the first time since it happened, I remembered opening the door for the strange man, and I remembered my father's words: Don't ever open the front door again.

Unknowingly, all my life I'd listened. I'd had the nightmares, seen the ghosts of the past, simultaneously romanticized big, scary men and pushed them as far away as I possibly could. I worked for a woman who sunk her fangs into her employees necks, locking them under her grip and swallowing the key. Reaching down her throat to retrieve it was my first act of rebellion against my indoctrinations. Moving out was my second.

As the person at my door knocked again, I felt my heart beat faster. I felt my chest constrict. Mommy and daddy weren't going to open it for me. And my life hadn't emulated theirs, so I didn't have a spouse to check the peep hole or a baby to make me brave. I only had myself. And that was enough.

I hope that's enough.

I didn't hesitate to go and answer it.

Anubis and the Three Bears

Keith Hoffpauir

When I was twenty-seven years of age, I was living in Colorado, A small town called Bailey that was about fifty-two miles west of Denver on Highway 285 at an elevation of 9,000 feet. My home was just below the peak of the mountain that it was located on. I had been living in a four-bedroom two bath, two story house, with a warp around a porch. When you stepped out of the living room door to the south of the house you were greeted by the tops of trees and a view that looked down into the valley below and out over to the ridge line on the other side of the valley.

At this point in time I owned a dog, not just any dog but a mutt. He was a half German Shepard, and his other half was Coyote. I dubbed him Anubis Vincent Hoffpauir in a strange ceremony that took place in the light of the full moon out on the deck overlooking the valley. Why did I do this? I do not know and cannot say why. Perhaps, I felt this dog, my dog, needed a naming ceremony, because by all that is unholy, I must be as extra as possible sometimes. Thus, with his name given Anubis was my constant companion.

He would go out during the day and sometime in the evening down to valley and like all dogs would find something to roll in before he would come back reeking of some form of foul, decay, and or death. He was smart enough to know his name, whether this was due to the naming ceremony in the moonlight or that coyotes are highly intelligent I cannot say why, maybe because that in certain native American myths the coyote was a creator god or a trickster, or both. However, Anubis was most assuredly not a creator god, though he may very well have had the trickster aspects either way he was smart. Anubis could tell what mood I was in based on how I called him, and how much of his name I used, determined how he returned to me. If I simply called for him by his first name, he would return head up, tail up and be happy to see me. However, if I called his full name out, he knew he was in trouble and would return as fast as possible with his head down and tail tucked as if to say, "Yeah I fucked up sorry about that please don't be mad." I was never mad with him, not even when I took back my sandwich he stole from my hand and ate it in front of him.

He would go with me on trips into the city, or when we walked around on the mountains, or down into the valley. It was one of these walks at the end of spring or early summer that Anubis and I had an encounter. We started early, leaving the house at sunup and hiked down into the valley. We had gone down to the creek, looked at the beaver dam, and checked out the area where they gnawed down some of the trees for their work. I had at this point decided to take a break in this clearing. I sat on a rock that was jutting out of the ground that had a clear flat space on it for me. I looked around and did not see Anubis. I called him and waited, after a few minutes, I called again this time using his full name. As his norm he came back head down, tail tucked, but this time he had followers. Three small fluffy brown bear cubs. Yes, this dog, this smart, yet stupid canine had decided to make friends with some bear cubs and thought to bring them along to go meet his companion.

The three bears, I do not know if they were male, female or a combination of both, were coming up to me with my half breed dog. I blame Anubis' coyote blood for all of this. He came to sit in front of me with a look of "I'm sorry, but hey I brought my friends." His friends were by no means shy about meeting me either. Then again young animals out in the wild have no reason to fear something they have not met before, and we humans have long been the interlopers in the domain of the wild. They played with my dog and would come and inspect me sometimes. It is odd that I have never really given any thought about being sniffed by a trio of baby bears. They really are dog-like in a lot of their interactions with the world around them. They have no boundaries when it comes to trying to sniff you out to get your scent or find what they are looking for that you may be hiding, like the ham sandwiches, hotdogs and Anubis meals, a snack for my dog fit for the god of the afterlife, that were packed away in my backpack. Eventually they caught the scent of my lunch and were not taking no for an answer when I would try to get them to leave me, or rather my backpack alone.

So, I divested myself of my goods. I pulled out the hotdogs, the ham and bread and Anubis snacks, if I must share my food, so does he, I mean they are his friends anyway. I would hastily eat a ham sandwich in between throwing slices of ham out into the area in front of me for my companion and his friends to eat. Once I had eaten my sandwich and could focus more on the cubs and Anubis, I took out the hot dogs. A bear will not hesitate to try and bite your finger to get to the processed goodness that is a hot dog. It is also funny as all get out when you toss a wiener, and it bounces off a bear cub's head to be caught on the rebound by another cub. The fight that ensued was amusing to watch, until a sound arose from across the distance from the tree line where Anubis and the cubs had come from. The roar was one that sounded as though it were calling out as if to say, "Where is everyone?" and it was not a small call, rather this was the sound you would hear coming from an adult with authority. The cubs heard the cry, and their little heads perked up, and they looked to the tree line. We were all looking at the tree line honestly frozen where we sat. It roared again and this time the cubs responded. Finally lumbering out of the forest and into the clearing she came. A very large brown bear. I can only assume this is a momma bear because when she saw the cubs with my dog and me sitting within a few feet she came running towards us.

I have mentioned before that bears can be very dog-like in how they respond to things. One of the things that I have learned aside from bears having pretty good noses is that bears, again like dogs, will chase things, especially if they are running away. So, when being charged by a bear, the advice that is given by the state every spring is to stand your ground. I was afraid, this bear easily outweighs me and is taller than I am if she stands to her full height, but I know if I run, I will be chased down and caught. As she closed the distance, I grabbed a hot dog and threw it. I did not aim; I just threw the wiener and bounced the meaty treat off her nose. This is when several things happened in rapid succession.

First momma bear stopped dead in her tracks, I do not know if this was due to the fact that she caught the scent of the hot dog, or if it was that this human had the audacity to her hit her on the nose with his meat stick, whatever the reason was, she stopped. Next Anubis ran up to the momma bear, again I do not know the animal thought process, if this was an attempt to protect me, or if he really wanted that hot dog, I cannot say with certainty. I like to believe it was out of a sense of loyalty. Standing before the momma bear, he started barking, adding to the confusion. Now it was time for the cubs to join this rapidly evolving circus. Two of the cubs ran up next to Anubis and started growling and huffing, communicating as bears do, while the third one had their priorities set on the hot dog that landed on the ground. I believe that cub is my spirit animal. When the situation at hand is crazy, the best course of action is to just walk off and find the food, but I digress.

Momma bear is now confused in every way she can be, a dog is barking at her, two of her children are yelling at her, and the third is gobbling down a hot dog that just bounced off her nose, and there is this human sitting on a rock just looking at scene in front of him. So, she did what any parent would do; she yelled. She roared so loud it seemed as though the entire mountainside went quiet afterwards. We all looked at her, she huffed and made some bear noises and turned her back to me and started to walk away, her cubs getting in line behind her to go back into the forest. Anubis barked some goodbyes and came to sit on the rock with me. Momma and the cubs disappeared into the tree line. I packed up as I processed what had just happened, ready to hike back home, happy that this was the end of my urine-filled adventure.

That is what I would like to say, but the bears had other plans. As soon as I take my first step, I hear the huffing and the footfalls of a little critter. I turned to see Anubis running to greet one of the cubs who for some reason, likely wanting to finish off the hot dogs I had left, decided to return. Followed by a second and then the third. All I can do is roll my eyes at this point and wait for the inevitable. It did not take long for momma bear to return after her kids who have decided to rebel against her wants and wishes. However, this time I was not staring down at a rage filled mother charging at me but more of a parent who has given up at this moment and decided to take the "L" and let the kids have their way. She came within six paces of where I sat up on my rock and sat down on the grass below. I felt for momma in this moment, because I have done the same thing with that dog of mine, and in the intervening years I also have come to understand that mother bear more as a parent myself. Momma came and settled herself down between me and the playful quartet of animals, and I decided to throw Momma a peace offering. I pulled out the remaining hot dogs and tossed them her way. After sniffing them she just ate them, though it looked like she swallowed them whole, and I guess after confirming I wasn't planning on moving towards her or her children, she settled down to wait for the kids to finish their play date, occasionally looking up at me when I moved or shifted from where I was at.

After about an hour, the animals were done. They had spent their time playing chase, some odd kind of hide and go seek, and some game where they would all go in different directions and bring back something they found, or dug up, but they finally came up to the rock. The cubs snuggling next to momma bear and Anubis finding his way up the rock to drink some water I had put into a bowl for him and then settle down next to me for some needed rest. More time passed and the animals stirred once more but this time we had to go. Packing everything I stood up; I made my way down from my perch with Anubis to begin the hike home. As I walked by momma bear the cubs came up and rubbed against me and their momma just looked over at me lazily. I guess at this point she decided I was not a threat to the kids like she had originally thought. I was able to reach down and pet the cubs and wish them all goodbye. Anubis barked a few times, and we departed. The hike home was uneventful, and we made good time. I never saw the cubs or momma again after that day, and as the years have gone by from time to time I still think about Anubis, my little coyote and all the trouble he brought to me that day and smile.

Have a Heart for Japan

Kadence Jack

Imagine someone stepping into your country and vandalizing your cherished sanctuaries and revered statues. Would you still offer them a warm welcome? Although I've yet to visit Japan, I've always admired the way its citizens respect cultural traditions and treasures. Japan stands out as one of the cleanest and most unique countries in the world.

During my high school years, I felt a profound calling to share my passion for Japanese culture, which led me to establish a Japanese Culture Club. What started as a humble gathering of enthusiastic individuals blossomed into a vibrant community space where I could express my deep love for this rich culture. It filled me with immense pride to witness others immersing themselves in the traditions and history that I cherished so dearly. There's something incredibly special about its culture that sets it apart from all other countries. My affection for Japan runs deep, even though I have never set foot in another country, my fascination began with my dad sharing glimpses of Japanese currency, stunning photos of Mt. Fuji, and enchanting cherry blossoms. The allure of this incredible country captivated me and sparked my interest in languages and ignited a passion that led me to delve deeper into its culture.

That interest motivated me to begin learning the language. Japan has always captivated me, and I'm eager for the day I can immerse myself in its traditions, culture, and everything that makes it so remarkable. Its heritage carries a distinctive charm—rich, vibrant, and endlessly intriguing to anyone who encounters it. The people embody a gentle and composed spirit, creating an inviting atmosphere. Much like anime, which showcases a stunning range of styles, the masterpieces of Mr. Hayao Miyazaki are bursting with life and vibrancy. His art flows beautifully, brimming with color that captures the very essence of his homeland. The energy he infuses into his creations is nothing short of magic. Conversely, Mr. Junji Ito explores the darker realms of horror, his work marked by chilling themes and striking tones that leave a profound impact. The stark contrast between these two remarkable artists is truly striking, perfectly embodying the concept of yin and yang. Each brings something extraordinary to the world of art, enriching it in their own distinctive ways. Even the music has a lively spirit, enchanting and captivating, creating a delightful experience for the soul. Like Mt. Fuji, it serves as a recognizable landmark for Japan, offering a sense of familiarity and comfort to those who encounter it.

It's truly disheartening to witness foreigners who show a blatant disregard for Japanese culture during their visits. Such disrespect can ruin the experience for others and tarnish the beauty and traditions that this country holds dear. It's perplexing to see some visitors behave like children, disrespecting the elderly and treating sacred spaces as playgrounds. I recently came across a video on social media of a woman riding the Hachikō statue as if it were an amusement ride. It infuriates me because it reflects a lack of understanding and respect. Why would anyone choose to act in such a foolish way? It certainly doesn't portray them in a positive light. It's unfortunate how some actions or perceptions can cast a shadow over all foreigners, making it seem as though they are the ones at fault, even when many haven't done anything wrong.

It's important to remember that stereotypes can harm everyone and that we should seek to understand and support one another, regardless of our background. It's disappointing also that an Australian man chose to film himself entering a women-only train carriage in Japan while calling himself a "women inspector." This kind of behavior shows a lack of respect for the purpose of these carriages, which are meant to provide a safe space for women who might be dealing with harassment (chikan). It's concerning that he disregarded these important rules and made other passengers uncomfortable. It's hard to understand why someone would think this would be acceptable behavior. This situation raises important questions about respect and awareness in shared spaces. It's heartbreaking to witness the decay of etiquette in a place known for its serenity. When people carelessly toss their trash on the ground as if it's acceptable behavior, it feels like a betrayal of everything Japan stands for. Smoking in prohibited areas? Ignoring the rules and recording things that should remain private? The noise and chaos on the trains—this isn't New York or any other city known for its hustle and bustle. When I encounter news articles that resonate with my views, it reinforces the necessity of sharing perspectives that contribute to valuable discussions. "According to AP news

Anti-foreigner sentiments and politicians are on the rise as Japan faces a population crisis. In this news, it talks about anti-foreigner sentiments. Japanese, as they struggle with dwindling salaries, rising prices, and bleak future outlooks, many Japanese are frustrated by these problems, though we are way too reserved to speak out. Mr. Kamiya is spelling them out for us, said Kenzo Hagiya a retiree in the audience who said, "foreigner problem is one of his biggest concerns." Also, according to "The Diplomat, "New fees are designed to limit the number of tourists, too. Beyond the sheer numbers of visitors, there's an increasing sense that their behavior is a problem. Japanese complain that tourists jaywalk, litter, curse, and otherwise behave in ways that are out of step with Japan's cultural norms. Officials are pushing a new framework for responsible tourism. In one famous example, local officials erected a fence in a desperate attempt to stop tourists from taking selfies with Mount Fuji in the middle of the road."

Japan is celebrated for its calm and gentle spirit, and yet, it seems that this respect is slipping away. If they keep moving in this direction, it's concerning to think that we might unintentionally close off access to this wonderful country for good. It would be truly sad to realize that our own decisions could lead to such an outcome.

Traveling is not just a luxury; it is a crucial privilege that comes with great responsibility. It should never be mistaken for entitlement, as the experiences and lessons gained through travel are invaluable and should be approached with gratitude and respect.

Before embarking on a journey to a new country, it is incredibly advantageous to engage in thorough research. Understanding local customs, traditions, and social norms can significantly enrich your travel experience. Taking the time to familiarize yourself with the country's cultural foundations—such as its greetings, dining etiquette, and festivals—will enable you to navigate social interactions more smoothly. For example, learning about traditional greetings can help you make a good first impression and connect with locals on a deeper level. Additionally, knowing what dishes are commonly served and their significance can enhance your appreciation when sampling local cuisine, whether it's enjoying spicy street food in Thailand or savoring rich pasta dishes in Italy. Furthermore, being aware of important cultural practices, such as dress codes or public behavior, can help you blend in and show respect, making your interactions with the locals more meaningful. Ultimately, this level of preparation transforms an ordinary trip into a memorable adventure filled with immersive experiences that you will cherish for a lifetime!

I want to sincerely apologize to the people of Japan for the disrespect shown by some foreigners. It pains me to see that there are those who do not take the time to understand and appreciate your rich culture and values. Please know that their actions do not reflect the feelings of all who visit your beautiful country.

I humbly ask for your understanding and want to assure you that many of us truly respect and admire Japan and its people. I genuinely hope to visit your lovely country someday and truly experience all the beauty it has to offer.

Works Cited

Ke, Bryan. "Australian travel vlogger slammed for going inside 'women-only' train carriage in Japan." Nextshark, September 13, 2023. https://nextshark.com/australian-travel-vlogger-backlash-women-only-train-carriage-japan.

"What's Japan's Problem with Foreigners?" The Diplomat. October 22 2025. https://thediplomat.com/2025/10/whats-japans-problem-with-foreigners/.

Yamaguchi, Mari, "Anti-foreigner sentiments and politicians are on the rise as Japan faces a population crisis." Apnews, October 25 2025, https://apnews.com/article/japan-xenophobia-immigration-sanseito-antiglobalism-trump-foreigners-358e5eb2b9d6bfe4814cac1b35557e1f

Short Fiction

Desire

Joseph Bernard

Trigger warning for themes of discrimination of women and male supremacy

Chapter 1: A Normal Happy Day

The sun shined through my window, gently kissing my face to wake me up. I left myself from the bed, stretching and yawning to this beautiful day. I get out of my bed and immediately go to my mirror; I try to make my hair in a way my boyfriend would love. He always said that having the hair covering my forehead is always a good choice, and in a way I do agree. I made sure to brush my beautiful brown hair and then tie it up in a ponytail. After that, I go over to my closet and pick out a wonderful yellow sundress. It was the perfect choice for this perfect Sunday.

I then headed downstairs to the kitchen, grabbing several ingredients to make my father and I some breakfast. As I cooked, my father came down from his room and greeted me, "Hey there, sweetie, how did you sleep last night?" I turned around and greeted him with my pretty smile, the smile that everyone says they love to see. "Oh, I had an awful nightmare last night, Dad, but I know it was all in my head," I answered him with glee. My father chuckled and said, "Well I am very happy to hear that my little girl is doing well." We then sat down and ate the breakfast I cooked for us. He talked to me about the plans we have for today. First, we go to church, then after that we go to, "Bob's Diner," and lastly, I will go with my boyfriend on a very special date. I was kicking my feet in excitement; I just can't wait to see him again!

After we ate the food that I cooked for us, my father and I got ready for church. I made sure to put on the heels my boyfriend Joseph loves to see. It was red with a bow on the tip of my shoe. I just squeal whenever I think of my Joseph; he's so handsome, and such a dork. Girls would tell me how jealous they are that he's mine, but he is. It feels wrong whenever I don't think of him. Oh right, I almost forgot that I must go to church with my dad. I hurried out of my room with my purse around my shoulder. My father smiled warmly when he saw me come down the stairs, "Ah, you look so lovely, Mary," he said as he landed a kiss on my cheek.

We went out to his blue car, I don't know what kind of car it is though, to me it's just a blue car. My Dad loves to talk about it to me, and I love to listen even though I have no clue what he is talking about. The drive to church was so peaceful and calm, just like every other day. Time seems to fly within that drive to the church, and once we made it, I saw my boyfriend. Joseph was so handsome and looked amazing in that black suit and tie. When the car stopped, I got out and ran to him, wrapping my arms around Joseph. He wrapped his arms around me too, making sure to cup his favorite part about me, or at least that's what he tells me. "Hey there Mary, how are you doing on this beautiful morning," he asked, squeezing where his hand is on me. I giggled when he touched me, Joseph is so funny when it comes to his hands. My Father was right behind us, giving his nod of approval.

We headed inside the church; we sat down on one of the pews close to the choir. I love sitting close to the choir, the singing is so beautiful to me. Joseph was still being so silly, squeezing my leg like he was excited for our date later today! The priest then came up to the table at the front of the church. Honestly, I wasn't really listening to what he was saying; I was just too busy thinking about Joseph. Gosh, he's so handsome. During the church ceremony, my Father got close to me and fixed my hair. "Sorry honey, it's just that your hair was a little off," he told me with a reassuring smile. I giggled when he told me that my Father can be so weird, but I don't mind. After all, I am his little girl even if I am already dating the best man around town.

Soon church would be over, it was long and boring anyways. Now it was time for us to go and get our grub. Me, my Father, and Joseph would head towards the nearby diner. The place was packed with people from the church, I think I even saw our priest here. We sat in the booth, with me sitting next to my dear boyfriend, Joseph. He put his arm around me when we sat together. My Father and Joseph were talking to each other, you know how guys are. I can't really talk to them unless they ask me something, otherwise I would just be a nuisance. I don't like being a nuisance to them though, I love them very much. I then felt something in my stomach, "Uh, Joseph dear, may I go to the back of the diner and relieve myself," I asked him. "Oh, of course Mary, just make sure to hurry up, okay?" Joseph said as he puts his arm back to his side.

I hurried to the restroom to take care of my problem; I tried to do it as quickly as possible. I felt a little pain when I did it, but it was all over. I checked the mirror after I used the mirror, to make sure I still look pretty and… wait, why is there a large stitch on my forehead? It's not a bruise or a scar, a full-on surgical stitch. Like as if my brain was opened and messed with. Oh god, why do I feel so scared, so wrong, so terrible. Why can't I remember when this happened? What's the earliest thing I can remember? C'mon, please give me something from five months ago. I can barely remember anything five months ago; anything before that is either faded or probably forgotten. When I found this stitch, I tried to remember my life, but I started to realize just what I had been doing. Why was I so fine with how my boyfriend touched me, and why did I even start dating him? I can barely remember why I even liked him in the first place. I need to find out what exactly happened to me.

Chapter 2: A Normal Happy Day?

I just realized that I was probably taking too long in the restroom. I fixed my hair and immediately went to the door. Once I opened it, I saw Joseph right there at the entrance of the women's restroom. "Oh, I was going to check up on you, are you okay honey?" He asked, his eyes never touching my face. I answered his question, "Oh yeah, everything is fine, Joseph." He took one quick look at my face, I tried to give him a quick smile, hoping Joseph didn't suspect anything. After what felt like minutes of him staring at my face, he shrugged and went back to our booth. I followed behind him, and once we made it, I sat next to my father. Joseph looked at me weirdly, like I was an actor in the wrong spot. My father didn't seem to mind though. "So, back to our conversation, Joseph, where do you plan to take my lovely daughter tonight?" My father asked, looking straight to Joseph's face, judging him. Oh shoot, I had a date with Joseph later. I really don't want to go with him, especially since I don't trust him that much. I mean, I barely know the guy and I am supposed to love him. Maybe I did know him before the scar, but I don't know. I just want to yell and scream at Joseph, demanding that he gives me an answer. Unfortunately, I am in a public space, and I would sound like a psycho if I blurted that out.

Joseph looked back at my father, "Oh I plan to take her to a scary movie, and after that I plan to… you know," he said with a smug face. My father laughed at his comment, I couldn't really understand why though. It's obvious what Joseph is talking about, and yet my own father is simply laughing. I don't really want to go with Joseph tonight, I need to find a way to pull myself out of this.

"Ah, well I know you two will have fun tonight," my father stated as he took a big sip from his drink. I finally decided to say something, "Actually, I am feeling kind of sick, could we perhaps… reschedule it?" It felt wrong to say anything like that to them, but at the same time it felt like I was doing something right. The two men looked at me with confusion, there was silence to my question. It was quite awkward. The restaurant kept going around us for what felt like hours, but really it could have been a few minutes. My father broke the silence with a cough and answered a question that was asked long ago, "Honey, are you alright?" I kind of felt awkward about it too; this entire thing is awkward. I opened my mouth, "I don't feel alright father." Joseph seemed kind of irritated; his plan for the night was ruined by me.

I feel like my stomach was turning and turning into knots. My mind feels so conflicted about all this, doing that, saying these things to them. I feel like I am destroying something that was beautifully built, like a statue of a woman. On the other hand, it feels necessary. One half screams for me to stop; the other begs to keep me going. Neither side seems evil, but one comes with a comforting familiarity, and the other promises that my life can be more than what I have. I can't decide what I want now, but I do need to figure out this scar first to fully figure out what happened to me, and why I can't remember.

We soon had our lunch; it was pretty tasty even though my time was ruined by my own discovery. Joseph waved me goodbye, and I gave a small wave back. My feelings for him are conflicted now. I have this feeling I love him, but I don't know anything about the guy. All I know is that I am supposed to love him a lot. Is this my real love, or is this a love forged onto my mind? Which is truth and which is fiction? Which emotion is mine, and which one was given to me? The ride home with my father felt longer than usual. I looked over to him and asked, "Father, is it okay if I am feeling better tomorrow, I could take the car?" My father replied, "No honey, you know you don't have a license. Besides, you really shouldn't have one, driving is a man's job." I was confused when he told me this. What makes driving a man's job? It's just a car. But he is a guy, and I don't really know how to drive a car. On the other hand, while it seems complicated, I think I can do it. I then decided to ask him, "So you trust me with cooking your foo-" My father then raised his voice, "Hey, don't talk back!" I shrunk from his demand; it felt weirdly natural to submit to his voice, and I hated it. Both sides of me did, but with conflicting problems. One side blames me, and the other is just screaming to continue talking back. What makes him think he can just shut me up? I can't talk back to him though; I don't want to make anything worse. That new side of my mind was telling me what it would do to my father, and it strangely made me happy in a dark way.

Once we finally made it back to our home, my father looked at me right in the face. "Don't talk unless I talk to you, cook dinner in a few hours, make sure to do your chores, after dinner bathe yourself and go to bed," he ordered to my face. It was stern, but not loud. There is some hint of frustration though; it feels almost as if it's my fault but splits as to why. We get out of the car and walk through the entrance of our home. What once felt like a warm welcome feels like a cold, begrudging hello from the home I have known for so long despite my memory going only for a few months ago. I go to the laundry room to do one of my many chores given to me by my father. His clothes were a variety of shirts for multiple purposes, loads of pants, and some disgusting briefs. God, how did these brown stains not break me out of my mind? When I eventually got to my clothes, they were the same. The same type of sundress over and over, the same type of socks over and over, and even the same type of underwear over and over. The sundresses were almost exactly like mine, with the only distinction between them all being the color. The colors were all light, though I did have some sundresses in darker colors. Is this really all I wore, or is this all my father wanted me to wear, or Joseph, or both? I don't think anyone would want to wear the same thing every day. Soon the laundry was finished, I quickly washed my hands after handling my father's dirty briefs.

Next up were the dishes; the activity itself felt like it was normal but also repetitive. Not repetitive as in doing the task once, but like I have every night. Every soap and water that touched my hands felt like a family member to me, like I have known this for a long time. Cleaning all this felt wrong too, but wrongness is new. A fresh emotion to this chore. The soap and water that feel like family now feel like they're hiding a dirty dark secret from me. Like my father, Joseph, and possibly like everyone else. Who do I trust with this forbidden knowledge I know? Who do I share this information with? Keeping it with me sounds like a good idea, but it'll feel so lonely. Even if I told someone, could they even keep it a secret if they tried their hardest? Are there other women in this town like me, or am I the only one? There's only one place I can go to find out, but not now. I need to appease my father and hope he doesn't find out about me.

I finished up the dishes, it took a while, but I managed. Each plate and bowl are stacked on each other inside the cupboards; every single utensil is properly placed in their correct spot. I can tell it's a little off than how I usually do it, but I don't mind that. What I do mind is if my father knew. Why do I care about what he thinks? I feel like that reason changed today but left how I interact with my activities mostly the same, to keep my father happy. I can't live like this anymore, I don't know if it's a life anyone would want, but it is one I really don't want. My father spoke loudly, a booming voice through the home, "Mary, where's the dinner? You know mother would have made it if she was still with us, God bless her soul."

"I'm on it, Father," I responded to his query. I walked to the fridge and peeked into it; I took some fruit and some cream cheese. I planned on making a fruit salad, all the food I have cooked involved meat, and I feel like making something different for tonight. I mashed the fruit, not too messy though. I wanted to make the collection into small pieces, and then I would use the cream cheese to mix it all together. After a bit, the fruit salad was finally done. I grabbed a bowl and placed some of it into it, I then brought the bowl to my father. My father was on the chair, he was wearing less clothes than before, wearing a white sleeveless shirt and underwear, it looked unwashed and disgusting. My father was watching the television, a game of men hitting each other to show who was stronger. At least that's what it looked like; I had no interest in sports. I don't know if that's something natural in me or forged onto me. "Here you go father," I said as I handed him the bowl. My father looked at it, but he wasn't happy. "Ugh, where's the meat? God, what're you broken?" My eyes widened in shock, "N-No, it's okay! I will make what you want." I watch my father carelessly drop the bowl to the floor. "I desire a hotdog with cheese and make it snappy. I wish your mother was here, she would have helped you much better!" My father exclaimed. I nod as I crouch down and pick up the bowl. I went to the kitchen and quickly made my father the hotdog he desired, tears ran down my eyes. I felt weak, I felt controlled, I felt like I missed not knowing.

After I cleaned the fruit salad on the floor, and made my father the hotdog he wanted, I ate my own salad. Despite being home with someone else, I felt alone. My problems are my own, and I realized I need to get out of this. I don't know how, but I will find my way out. I enjoyed what I made, and I cleaned up the stuff I used to cook. I walked up the stairs, stepping into my bedroom. I disrobed myself and used a towel to wrap around my body. I walked to the bathroom, ready to clean and cleanse myself of the dirt that laid on my body. I turned the water on; it was hot and steaming. In my head, it would be like cooking myself. Maybe I can cook the pain away and turn it into a soup of some kind, transforming my pain into something useful. I soon turned the water off; the tub was half water with steam coming out, and the other half was missing me in it. I dropped the towel and slowly entered the water. It hurt but was also soothing. A soothing pain. I think long and hard about everything this day brought, especially the discovery of a secret about me that I didn't know, but others might have known. It haunts me, these past five months being the only thing I know, the only thing I have ever known really. I can't even remember my own mother. I should be sad, I should be crying. I can't remember someone who I should love but I can't. I barely know her. I don't even know when she died, how, or even her last words. Why do I not even shed a tear for a mother that I feel like I should care for but have no clue who she is? That's not all, everything about my life feels controlled by others. The way I dressed, the way I cooked, the way I talked, maybe even my own thoughts started to feel like they were never mine but simply things that needed to be forced into me. Shoved into my own brain like a sick experiment and I was the end result. It might sound messed up, but I hope I am not the only one because this feels so much worse if I am alone in this situation. I rub the scar on my head; it feels wrong to touch, wrong to know, two different wrongs, the one wrong that says it's forbidden to know, and the other wrong that says it's forbidden to have this done to me.

I finished up my bath, cleaned my mouth, and then drained the water. I put the towel around me and headed off to bed. I made a decision to listen to the new side I have gained. I don't know if the other was forced into my mind, or if it was a way to cope with it all. Either way, I need to know, and I might have to leave. I can't do that with this more submissive voice in my head. I then fell asleep.

Chapter 3: A Not So Normal Day

I woke up from my bed, pushing specific thoughts of going back to a normal life to the back of my mind and inviting the new rebellious thoughts. I looked through my closet, seeing that it's still the same as yesterday. I can't show that I know what I know just yet, so I decided to put on the red sundress as not a sign of rebellion, but as a disguise. I walk over to the bathroom, looking in the mirror. I made sure it looked good within my father's eyes, even if I hate how it looks. It looked the same as yesterday, and the days before. I then walked down the stairs and made my way to the kitchen. I started to cook the type of meal my father would love the most, a bacon and cheese sandwich. I work hard on it, making sure it's as good as possible, that way my father would be more easily convinced to let me go out. Why must I go out? I need to find my way to the hospital, sneak into the building, and figure out the truth of my scar that lays on my head. My father came down, a loud whistle escaping his mouth, "Oh boy! I'm smelling something good!" I put on a nice and kind smile, I don't know if it would pass as a smile, but if it's not convincing then I hope my father won't care about it. He sat down at the table, "Thanks for the delicious breakfast honey, really made it up for yesterday!" My father exclaimed as he began to wolf down the meal. I sat down at the table, having a bowl of the fruit salad I made for myself yesterday. I eat slowly, watching my father consume the sandwich without a care in the world. The poor sandwich was never cherished in my father's hand; he simply saw it as something to use to satisfy his own hunger and fill his own belly. It reminded me of my own predicament oddly enough.

Once my father devoured the sandwich, I stopped eating and asked, "Father, I know that you don't let me go out that much, but I honestly believe that for today you should. I was hoping to buy a new hat, would that be acceptable?" My father pondered this for a moment, and answered, "Sure, how about I drive you there an—" I cut him off before I could finish, "But father I would rather go alone." My father seemed angry at me, "Don't you dare interrupt me young lady. I pay for everything around here, don't you know? I pay for the food, the bed, the plumbing, everything! Interrupting me means you don't respect me! Do you respect me, Mary?" I nod, not showing a sign of fear, but deep down I just want to cower and try to quell his anger. I can't make him angry, but I don't want to show my weakness either. "I apologize father, I didn't mean to make myself sound like I disrespected you; I just simply wish to go out by myself." My father raised an eyebrow, like he was thinking. A smirk then appeared, "Fine then Mary, although you don't have a driver's license so you will have to walk there." I finished my meal, "That's okay father, I can handle it."

I put on some makeup and gathered my things, ready to walk my way to hospital since I have too. I leave the house and look around. It's strange that I have just noticed how every house looked similar to each other. It's almost like it is trying to replicate an idea of perfection. I walked down the street, keeping my bag to myself as I headed towards the hospital. Despite my memory loss, I do remember the general layout of the town. As I walk, I see people who are just out living their lives. The women do seem happy, but I can tell it's a forced happiness, or maybe it is just me projecting my own feelings onto them. The men are around, ordering their women what to do. I can see how easy of a life that can be when I am now looking on the outside. With no ability to think for oneself, one may not worry about the problems. That doesn't mean it's a good life though; it takes away the humanity that was once there and replaces it with something more. I don't have enough for myself to make an answer, but seeing this stuff really gets me to think about my own life for the past five months. I know I have already thought all of this over, and already my decision, but I can't help but think how simple and easy life was without knowing.

I then finally got closer to the hospital, although I am not there yet. I look around and see the different stores; they sell stuff like candy, electrical machines, and clothes. I was tired of this dress I always wore, so I checked my purse to see if I had any money. I had lots, probably from my father. I headed inside a store named, "God's Gracious Gifts," the store was filled with multiple different outfits. Most were dresses, though there were some that stood out. Skirts and blouses stood out to me, but I think I laid my eyes upon the long-sleeved shirt and some short pants, I think they are just called shorts though. I took them and tried them on; I liked how I looked. I don't care if anyone likes how I look, at this very moment what I care about is if I like how I look and I very much do. I put the sundress on a hanger in the changing room and left it. Before I walk out, I make sure my hair is hiding my scar. I walk out of the changing room and head to the counter. The young man there looks at me, I don't really mind him looking at me as much as I did with Joseph, although I do mind where his eyes are laid. "That'll be $50.65 ma'am," said the young man with a high-pitched voice. I looked through my purse, and thankfully I had enough money. I gave it to the young ma'am, and after that he handed me a receipt for it.

I walked out of the store, feeling more confident than ever. Honestly, I was pretty happy, even if it was a little more revealing than my sundress, or maybe it's as revealing just backwards? Who cares, besides me, of course. I then found my way to the hospital. When I walked in, there were a few people talking. I heard some nurses speaking. One nurse had red hair, and the other was blonde. I sat down, listening in to their conversation secretly. The red head was speaking, "So we have to find this girl named Mary? Uhm... she's the one who always wears that sundress right?" The blonde groans and rolls her eyes, "Ugh, I'm so tired of this, it feels like this type of stuff happens all the time. We should be quick though; we have done this kind of stuff plenty of times." I can't believe my new state of dress saved me from whatever the hospital wants me for. Although, what they are talking about sounds suspicious. Why do they want me, and furthermore what does this place plan for me? I dare not ask, for I fear revealing myself within this disguise. I decided to go up to the counter, maybe I could find some answers there. The doctor at the counter looked up at me, "Ah what're you here for? Broken bones, an illness, maybe you need some special fixing?" I shook my head, "I heard we are looking for a woman named Mary, do you perhaps know why?" The doctor sighed and answered, "Poor girl broke out of her place. Now we need to find her and fix her up good as new. Her father called us earlier; he suspected it as such." I nodded, but within my head I was terrified.

I left the hospital, determined to find answers, but I know I can't go any further in the hospital without a better disguise. I went into the alleyway to think, but then I saw something horrible. On the ground was a brunette woman, her nurse outfit was dirty, blood spilled from underneath her skirt, the neck with two handprints on them, and her eyes empty. I wanted to throw up when I saw her, poor woman. I can't comprehend what happened, but I know it must be something horrible. I looked around and decided to drag her corpse into the deep shadows of this very alleyway. "I know this is not what I should do, but I need to. I am sorry for what I will do to you." We exchanged clothes, I made sure to clean her outfit as best as I could. I put on her nurse outfit, it was a little too tight, but I will try to do what I must and then I'll come back to give her a proper burial once I am done.

Chapter 4: A Dark Day

I entered the hospital through the employee only entrance, I tugged on my outfit since it felt pretty tight. The doctors and other nurses pass by as I go down the hall. I am trying to look for a map, or some way to figure out where I am going. I can't really ask anyone where to go; it would make me look out of place. It could even reveal who I am, or maybe not. Either way, I can't let anyone be suspicious of me. I think I found my way to the break room, so I decided to walk in and take a seat. I was so tired of walking all day,

I know this might not be the best time, but my feet are killing me.

Two people walked in, a doctor and a nurse. The doctor walked over to the coffee machine; the nurse stood to the side and was smiling. The doctor saw me, "Hey, you know it's no time for a break!" He walked over to me quickly, "Come with me woman, I'll need help with a patient." I wanted to just ignore him, but I already know that not listening to him may make me look like I don't belong. I nodded and forced a smile on my face. He looked at me up and down and gave off a gross sly smile. Me and the other nurse left the break room with the doctor.

The doctor took us both to a room with a man sitting on a chair, and next to him is a woman laying down on the bed. The man got up and shook the doctor's hand eagerly. "Oh, thank the Lord, you're finally here! I found this girl breaking the rules we have laid out within our town. You must fix her!" exclaimed the man as he pointed to the woman sleeping on the bed. The doctor nodded and asked, "What did you catch it doing?" The man pulled out a magazine with some nice-looking woman on it, "I caught the woman looking through this magazine I own, it wasn't shocked by the pictures like a woman should, it was admiring the pictures." The doctor gave out a heavy sigh, "One of those, huh? Don't worry, we will fix this broad up in a jiffy. Just wait outside." The man nodded and walked out. The doctor pushed beside the hair covering her forehead, exposing her scar. The same scar I have, on almost the exact same spot too. The doctor looked at me and the other nurse, "Hold down its arms, I am going to make this woman just as perfect as it should be."

I gave out a small quiet gulp as I held down her right arm, and the other nurse held down the woman's other arm, a smile still on her face. The doctor leaned down and slowly cut the stitches off, which woke up the woman. She started to scream and cry loudly, her body was flailing around, she was trying to get out. I wanted to help her so badly, but I couldn't get myself caught so I had to sadly watch the woman cry out for help. The doctor pulled out some duct tape and crudely covered her mouth, "Be quiet, I can't fix you if you are screaming." The woman's face was clearly angry; her muffled screams can be heard through the tape. The doctor then pushed a scalpel into her head; the woman's face contorted from anger to shock and pain. Tears ran down her face as the doctor carefully cut open her head; I twinged as I watched the doctor hurt the woman by breaking into her head. The doctor then pulled out a tweezer and pushed that into the woman's head. She started to kick her legs as the doctor continued to mess with her brain, you can hear everything from that head, every fluid and brain matter either being cut or moved. The macabre seen before my eyes made me want to vomit. I saw the doctor pull something out of her head, causing the woman's screams to grow even louder, as loud as they ever have been through that tape over her mouth. Then, the woman stopped. She stopped screaming and stopped fighting. Her body was limp; her eyes were just as empty as the nurse from the alleyway. The doctor kept working though, not minding the fact that he may have possibly a dead woman on the bed of this hospital. He kept on poking, cutting, moving stuff in her brain from that slit on her forehead. The doctor ripped off the tape on her mouth, not caring for her safety at all. The woman soon moved a little, a smile then appeared on her face, it looked forced as if it was out of her control. The doctor finally finished messing with her head; he placed the utensils he used on a nearby metal tray. He then stitched her head back up and wiped her head clean. "Finally perfect," said the doctor as he looked at the woman who had lost herself.

Me and the other nurse let go of her arms, and then the woman sat up. The man from before came back into the room, making his way over to the doctor and shook his hand, "Oh thank God, thank you for curing the woman, Doctor!" The doctor scoffs and looks in the man's eyes, "Right, I am always happy to help bring these women back to their senses." I stood there uncomfortably in the area filled with superiority complexes. The doctor turned his attention to both me and the other nurse, "Well then, off you two. You have other responsibilities!" Me and the other nurse headed out of the room.

I decided to try and find my way around the hospital, a dumb decision, but what else can I do? I come across a large window with babies on the other side. Some babies had blue blankets, while others held onto pink blankets. The babies were within their own cribs, and the cribs each displayed a name. Each crib for the ones holding blue blankets had names that sounded more masculine: Matthew, Mark, Luke, and John. There was a variety of names for the ones holding the blue blankets, however the ones holding the pink blankets had only one: female. That was the only thing displayed on their cribs, female. It's disheartening that those with the pink blankets were reduced to such a name, these poor girls who are so new to the world already were considered the same way as any other woman is seen here in this town. I couldn't stay any longer, so I had to leave those babies.

My short time in this hospital may haunt me for a really long time. Are men really this capable of being so evil and seeing us so lowly?

I then found the room I was looking for, the file room. Finally, I can now find out the truth. I already know most about the events I have seen in this hospital that have shown me. What I want to know is what happened to me specifically. I found the file drawer that related to not only past patients, but also anyone with a first name starting with an M. It took a while considering I had to look through a lot. I then picked and prodded each and every file, trying to find my name. Mabel, Maggie, Magnolia, Manny, Maple, Mary. I finally found my own name. I opened it up.

This wasn't my first time finding out the truth, no, this is the fifth time. My first brain surgery was dated five years ago. I was shaking, I wasn't like this for five months, I was like this for five years. Stuck in this town with a broken mind, living it with men who value me more as a body than a person. I had to live in a town with other women possibly as equally broken as I am. I started to cry, sobbing on the floor. I don't know if I can take it. The truth hurts, but the worst part was within the files. The one behind not only the first one but behind them all was my father. I kind of thought it would have been Joseph, but it was my father who ordered the first one all along. Why did he do this to me? I want to fix this town so badly, but I am just one woman who has no idea what or who I am dealing with. I could break all the women out, but how would I even do that? What if the men have a countermeasure against it? I decided I must leave, it's cruel to leave all the women behind me, but I can't do anything.

I made my way out of the hospital, finding the corpse I hid away. We switched clothes again; I dusted off the dirt she had on herself. "I am so sorry I took your clothes; I am so sorry this all happened. I don't know your name, fellow woman, but may I call you Eve?" I closed Eve's eyes, hoping she may rest in a comforting warm afterlife better than this hellhole of a town. This vile, disgusting town that we were unfortunately born into. A place that I can't fix, that I must leave broken just like how it broke me.

Chapter 5: A Eventful Day

I left that alleyway with my heart sank low, I am an entirely different person, and I am so tired too. I found an abandoned building; it looked completely dilapidated. When I walk into the place, I can hear echoes of the past. There are papers that mention women's suffrage; tables and chairs were broken all around, and a few broken bats and clothes on the floor. I walked up the stairs, all the way to the attic. Up there I see another corpse. She was a woman, but unlike the last corpse this one wasn't as defiled. Instead, her head had a hole in it and nearby was a revolver and a bag of ammo. I examined the gun; it had six chambers, and five of them had bullets. I don't know what this woman was planning to do with all this ammo, but I know her pain. She must have known the truth just like me, the truth of our lives within this town. Her corpse gave me a third answer, suicide. I ponder the idea, if I am dead, I could leave this place forever and never look back. I gave it some thoughts, but ultimately, I decided not to. I want to live, but I want to be myself when I am living. I will save this gun as a way to defend myself, to attack, and if I have to…to end myself if needed. I sat down close to her, despite her being dead I pet her head hoping I could give her soul comfort in the afterlife.

It was for a couple hours of resting close to a dead woman, my mind and body are calm despite the unnerving circumstancesIamin.Igetupandgodownstairs,Ilookwithineachroom, looking for something soft. I found a heavy blanket in a child's room, and I took that blanket back to the attic. I lay the blanket on the dead woman, acting as trade for her ammo and gun. I take the ammo bag and place the bag inside. I walk out of the building, having a new goal. I am going to see Joseph and get him to speak the truth. I could go to my father, but I am too afraid to face him.

I walk down the streets of this town; I already have a mental map of how to get to Joseph. I think about what I should do when I get to his home, all I want to do is just kill him just like every other man in this town. My mind races with the possible ways I could make him scream and cry for what he and my father have done to me. I carry the bag with the gun and ammo in my left hand, gripping it to secure myself. I won't let this weapon of my hope go, it's my only hope. I see the men on the street, I have to stop myself from pulling the gun out and just shooting them, I have to keep my true real goal in mind, to find Joseph, talk to him, possibly kill him, and leave for good.

I stomped on over to his home; memories of my fake self play in my head, showing me being happy in his arms. But I know I, the real Mary, don't feel anything for him. The one who held those feelings was a fake Mary I was forced to pretend to be, but she is dead and buried while I am alive. I don't know if I am back to the original Mary, or if I am just some new one but that does not matter, I am me and I will choose what I will do before I leave this town for good. I go up to Joseph's door and knock on it. I pull the revolver out of the bag, ready for what I will do next.

Joseph answers the door, opening it up. "Oh Mary! Are you here for me?" asked Joseph, trying his best to look desirable. I point the gun to his face; Joseph's face transforms into someone who is terrified. "Yeah, I am here to see you, 'dear,'" I said sarcastically as I walked into his home, pointing my revolver at him all the time. I make Joseph close the door and guide him to his chair. I sit away from Joseph, always holding my gun towards him. "I want to know something Joseph, why would you go along with all of this? Is it because it benefits you, are you just this evil, why are you exactly like this? Why are all the men like this?" Joseph seemed stressed; his breathing was getting heavier, "I-I don't know! I am just a guy who lives here! How should I know?" I stood up, "Okay, then let me change the question: why do I and all the other women here have these scars?" Joseph's eyes darted around, seeking for a way out of this predicament, "Well, I don't know if you know this, but women are meant to serve men, it is a problem that women forget most of the time." Joseph said it like it was so normal, I almost let my guard down, but it was clearly enough for Joseph to grab a vase and throw it at me. I shot at the vase, which not only broke it, but it also hit Joseph's leg.

Joseph lays on the ground screaming in pain; he holds onto his leg. "Fuck! It hurts so much!" He stifled and cried on the floor, as I stood over him. My gun still pointed at Joseph. "Joseph, you shouldn't have done that," I said as I clicked the gun; the next shot was ready. "Now I want to know something else. Why have me love you? Why did you want me to love you, even if you might have known I didn't feel that?" Joseph looked around uncomfortably, "I don't know… I guess I like the idea of making a woman who doesn't feel those things and reverse them?" There was silence in the room. For a few minutes, I just looked at him. "Where are the car keys?"

Joseph gulped and asked, "Would I live if I tell you where they are?" I tilt my head, thinking about it. I then answered the question Joseph asked, "Maybe, maybe not. Your chances of seeing the morning sun will rise, but maybe not completely." Joseph nodded quickly and pointed to the table. "It's on the table, I promise just please don't kill me!" He cried like a baby as tears of terror ran down his cheeks. These men act so superior, but once a woman has more power right in front of them, they would cower. I opened the drawer under the table, and Joseph told the truth. I grab the keys and look back at Joseph, crawling away from me. I stomped back and shot his other leg. "Getting away from your victim? How cowardly." He cried out louder with his other leg shot, "I-I am the victim, you bitch! You come in here with a gun and shoot your boyfriend? I am the victim!" I rolled my eyes, "Do you think I care if you see yourself as the victim, Joseph?"

I then forced Joseph to look me in the eyes, "For five years I have been a completely different person, and every time I break free, I am brought back to that life forced upon me. I never had a choice in anything. The food I ate, the clothes I wore, the way I talked, the person who I love, and what I even thought! You are the many people who forced me and several other women to live like this in this god forsaken town! You think you're the victim? Well then, I will make you one!"

I then shot Joseph in the face, not allowing him to say anything to me. I didn't want him to say anything else, just stay dead. A man who continued and benefitted from my mind being contorted and distorted just like the other women in this town. I hate Joseph, I hate all the men in this town. I looked around the kitchen for a match, and once I found it, I used one of the matches to start a fire within the house. A symbolic gesture to the men that they will fall just like Joseph one day.

I left the house as it was in flames, the fire burned brightly and warmly. Killing should make someone feel bad, but for me killing Joseph made me feel better. Not perfectly better, but I felt like my justice has been sent. I know Joseph is burning in the hellfire below. I get inside his car and start the engine, ready to leave this place for good. My final night will be the second most eventful night of this town, and I hope the most eventual night this town would have would be its collapse.

Chapter 6: The Final Day

I got inside the car Joseph once owned, it's mine now though. My escape from this town. I put the keys in the car, and I will admit it was a little hard to learn how to drive this car. It's only because I was never taught how to drive though, not even as practice. I eventually learned enough to get myself out of there, slowly getting out of his driveway and then speeding up on the road. I almost crashed into a couple of homes, almost being the key word. I didn't care if the people saw me driving recklessly, but I did hope that they wouldn't follow me. It was a little hard finding my way around the town. It was easy enough to get myself to the hospital but leaving the town felt like a maze. I decided to just go down one direction after driving around for a bit. I would make a turn whenever I can, but I always go back in the same direction no matter what. I found the hospital on the way, and I know I need to keep going, but I need to help someone here.

I get out of the car and make my way to the back alley of the hospital. I find Eve placed exactly where I left her. I pick her body and take her back to my car. I gently placed her in the backseat. I don't know this, and all I know about her is that she is dead, but I do know she deserved a better death than this. I lay a blanket I found in the trunk on her, hopefully her soul will be warm when we leave this town. I get back into the car, and start driving again. I would sometimes look back at Eve, hoping that maybe what I am doing is helping to make up for what I have done.

I can see the sign to the town, which meant I was almost out of here. The sign said, "You are now leaving Christopher Rock, thanks for your stay!" This is it; I am almost out of here. That's what I thought, until I heard a gunshot followed by one of the tires popping. I lost control of the car; it steered off the road and flipped over. I wasn't knocked out, thank God. There was broken glass everywhere, I felt fire close by, and I looked at Eve who was now laying on the door. I was able to unbuckle myself, and crawl out of the car. I grabbed the gun for self-defense, or for suicide. I then heard a voice, "Mary, don't make me do this. Just give up quietly and everything will be alright." It was my father; he was here for me. I crawled slowly and quietly, hoping he wouldn't see me. My father yelled out, "You know what's best for you, Mary, I know what you did to Joseph. You think you can get away with that? You can, but there's only one way and that's getting your brain fixed!"

I hid in the tall grass, continuing to listen to my father as he kept searching for me. "Mary, I don't want to do the same thing I had to do to your mother, it would break my heart. Just show yourself and give up!" I slowly got closer, I wasn't going to talk to him, I can't talk to him. I can't let him convince me to give up. My father then turned around and saw me. "Mary, get up from the grass," he ordered. I slowly, surely, took my time getting up as deliberately and as carefully as possible, and then I shot his knee. The surprise shot left my father surprised, and in pain. He dropped the large gun as he held onto his knee. "M-Mary, you are so broken, Mary! Shooting your own father? How could you! You left behind your godly purpose as a woman and accepted the Satan into your life! You know deep down, God wants you to be submissive an-" I shut him up by shooting my father in the face.

I wasn't done yet though; I walked closer to him and stood over my father's face. I pointed the gun to his face. Bang, bang, bang, bang. I ran out of bullets, but not ammo. I quickly got the bag from the car and reloaded my revolver. I then returned to the position. Bang, bang, bang, bang, bang, bang. I then reloaded my gun. Bang, bang, bang, bang, bang, bang. I then reloaded my gun. Bang, bang, bang, bang, bang, bang. I then reloaded my gun. Bang, bang, bang, bang, bang, bang. I tried to reload my gun, but I ran out of bullets.

I climbed into the car and tried to pull Eve out of my car. I carried her corpse with me, leaving the town for good. I never looked back at that moment, carrying Eve in my arms. Eventually, I figured I got far enough. I sadly had no shovel, but I found some flowers. I laid Eve on the bed of flowers, hopefully these would treat her so much better than what kind of life God gave us. I even left the blanket with her. I gave her one final hug, and left Eve to sleep with the flowers. I already missed her, even though I never knew her.

As I kept walking, I got tired, hungry, thirsty, just feeling like I can't keep going. The road I was walking along had another connecting to it. I saw headlights from the side road, and the car seemed to stop when it saw me. The car door opened and out came a woman, she was beautiful, like an angel of some kind. I couldn't understand what she was saying, I was too tired to listen or talk. Instead, I fell into her arms, and she caught me in those strong arms of hers. I could feel her carrying me back to her vehicle, laying me in her backseat just like I did with Eve. I could feel the bumps on the road as my tired body lay in her car. I felt like I was being rocked away, like a baby in a crib. My eyes would then close, this entire day being the most eventful I ever have been in.

I woke up in a bed, a hospital bed. I started to freak out, am I back in the town? I thought I left, I thought I finally got out of here. I started to shake violently and crazy like an animal. A doctor then came in, but this doctor was different from other doctors I saw in my life. This doctor was a woman, like me. "Are you okay? What's wrong?" asked the doctor, trying to calm me down. It was pretty successful, replacing my fear with confusion. "Um…where am I?" I asked the doctor, looking up at her. The doctor started to write something down on her notepad, "You are in Caduceus Hospital ma'am." I sat up slowly, "Oh, I meant the town name?" The doctor's eyes widened, "Oh sorry, this isn't a town; it's a city. You are within the city of Hey-Soos." I nodded; I have heard of a city before, but it was mostly bad stuff. My heart started to beat faster when I saw a man, he was across the room from me, laying on a bed. I think the doctor noticed my nervousness; she patted my shoulder, “Hey, what’s wrong? You’re not looking alright.” I pointed towards the man, “W-What’s he doing here?” She looked at the man and scratched her head, “He broke a leg this week, do you know him or..?” I shook my head from side to side; I had no idea what she was talking about. Of course I had no idea. Since I was scared out of my life, the doctor decided to take me out of the room.

The doctor took me to see a “There-a-pist,” whatever that is. I was told to just talk to them about anything, and so I did. It took a while, and turns out I have androphobia, or the fear of men. When I told the “There-a-pist,” what happened, she didn’t believe me. However, she did say that I don’t look like I am lying. Later that day, I would be let out of that hospital, and soon my new life would start. A life that might be harder, but it will be my life. Not controlled by some men, or Joseph, or my father, or anyone. Me, it will all be me.

Now the real question was, where to start. I found a job listing, saying they need some chefs.

Epilogue: A New Day

It has been two years since I left that town, I was able to learn a lot of stuff by myself. I work at a restaurant as a chef, and if everything goes to plan, I might even own the place. I go to a therapist like every week; my past still haunts me. I can never truly run away from it. I thought I could solve my trauma and get rid of it. I don’t think I can, but I can learn to live with it. About my androphobia, while it is not completely gone, I have been getting better. I just have to keep reminding myself that I am safe here, that I won’t go back.

I walked to my apartment door; there was a newspaper on the floor. I picked it up and headed inside, and there was my roommate, Abigail. I found her while I was working, and decided to become roommates, although I do hope it can be more than that one day. “Oh, hey Mary, are you back from work?” Asked Abigail as she laid on the couch. Abigail was still studying for her college exams, her head in that Bible. I sat next to her, putting my feet on the coffee table, “Yeah, work was good though.” I pulled up the newspaper and looked through it. There was the usual stuff, but something caught my eye. It was Christopher Rock, the town I ran from two years ago. The entire place burned down yesterday; none of the authorities know why though. I was shocked, happy, but also shocked. It brought back memories, memories I tried to suppress. Abigail saw me, "Hey Mary, you don't look so good?" I got up, "I'm fine Abi, just give me a moment alone," I said as I left Abigail and headed inside the bedroom. We had our beds on different sides of the room.

I looked at the ceiling as I laid on my bed, and one of the most prominent memories I have is my father. I think my father genuinely loved me, but maybe he was misguided in some manner? My feelings for him are conflicting. I love him, but I hate him. I miss him, but I am also glad he is gone. I loathe him, but I want his touch. It's all so hard to deal with. I hear the door open; Abigail lays next to me. "It's okay Mary, they're gone," said Abigail, petting my hair and making me feel alright.

I think back upon that town too much, too much for it to be healthy. I can't let it go, even if I want it to. My life is my own now, and even if it was easier back then I can't go back. All I hope for is that burned down town are two things. That the women there are alive and can be themselves, and that something better will be built on top of it. If there is a God, please grant me that wish.

Divided

Jocelyn Rico

"Quién soy?" Carmen wondered every day, a question she could never answer in English or Spanish. Balancing school life and home life had always made Carmen feel divided in her world. She was a first-generation college student trying to navigate her way through college. At school she was a regular student. She maintained good grades and was very involved in extracurriculars, but nobody noticed the struggles she faced at home.

Although she would never fully admit they were struggles—maybe "setbacks?" As much of an accomplishment as it was for her and her family, it was a lonely path. Her parents had no idea how to support Carmen during her time in college. She relied on her advisors to guide her through financial aid applications and registering for her classes. The only advantage Carmen carried with her was that she had to grow up too soon.

Since she was a little girl, she had translated documents for her parents, who spoke very little English. She'd translated at the doctor's office and to adults since she was able to talk. While writing her American Literature final about the truth of the American dream, she received a call from her mom—"hola mija me puedes decir lo que está diciendo el doctor?" Having to stop what she was doing, she spoke to the doctor and translated to her mom.

A week later she got a screenshot from her dad of a text message from his boss—"mija me puedes decir lo que me dijo?" Again Carmen had to translate the message for her dad.

One of her least favorites was translating birthday cards because of how long the messages were. But when she did, her parents gathered around to listen while their faces lit up like children listening to a story. It made her happy that she was able to translate, but she felt guilty for being a little annoyed. *Why do I feel bad about helping them*? she wondered. *They depend on me, but sometimes I just want to feel like more than just their translator*.

Carmen was raised to be the voice for her family, to help them succeed in the country her parents had immigrated to before she was born. That itself was too much pressure. Carmen had to be good enough to make her parents' sacrifice seem worth it—something she felt her peers might not understand. The constant shift between her situations was causing her to go through an identity crisis, feeling she didn't belong on either side.

Sometimes Carmen wondered who she really was. At school, she was just another student who blended in. At home, she was the bridge between two worlds, losing her way on both sides.

Her parents smiled as they heard her perfect English being spoken, as if they'd realized they had accomplished their dreams of giving Carmen a better life. Although she struggled silently, they thought their daughter was becoming everything they couldn't be. They couldn't see how that "perfect" English sometimes felt like a wall between them. Despite the challenges, the only thing Carmen knew herself to be was the translator.

Maybe one day it'll be something more.

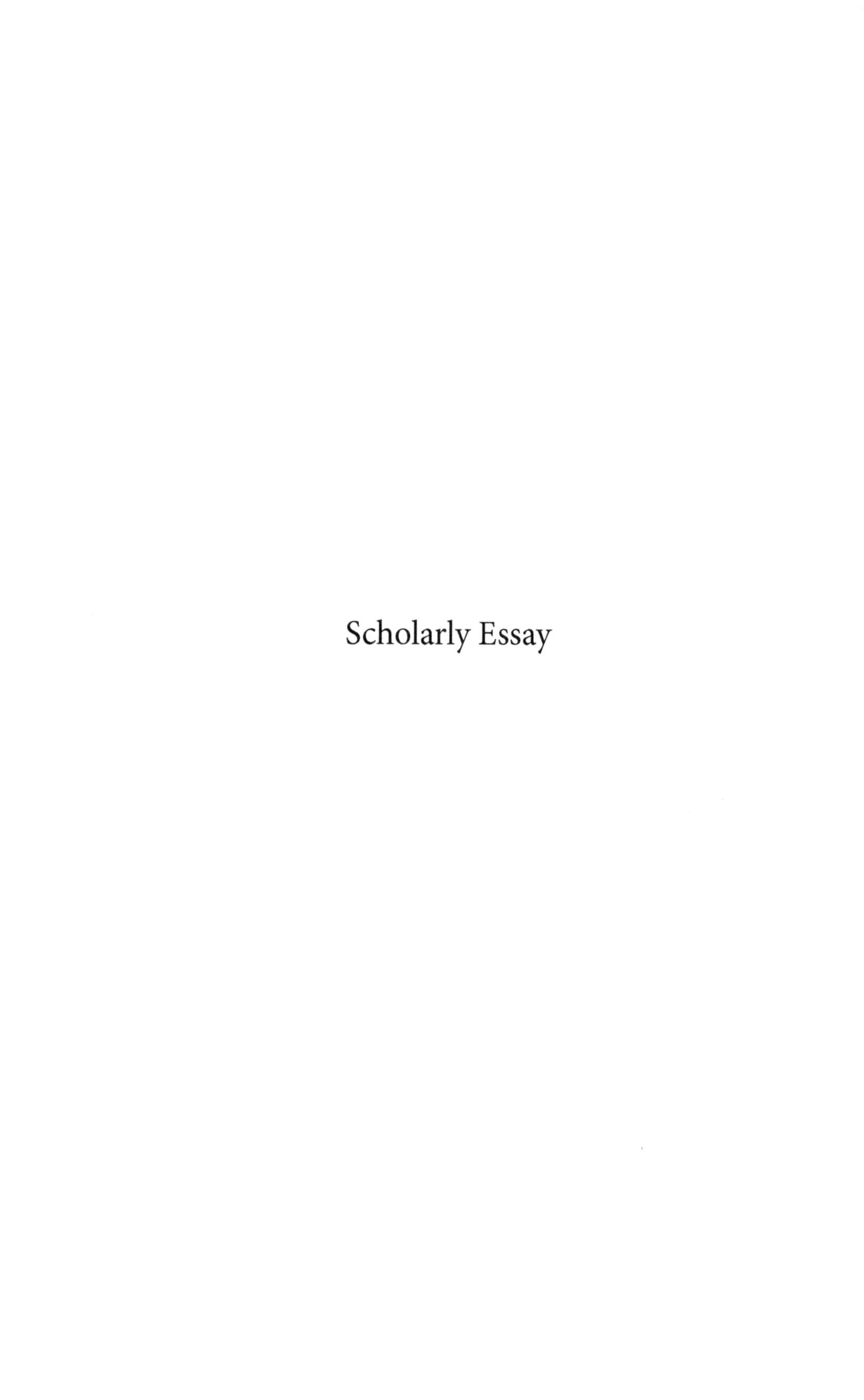

Scholarly Essay

Freud in *The Metamorphosis*: The Psychology of Surrealism

Mae Bradley

After The Great War, populations suffered devastation beyond imagination. While pro-war propaganda persuaded fathers, brothers, and sons to sacrifice themselves in the name of their countries, the harsh consequences of prolonged battle revealed themselves to the masses. As a result, discontented activists and artists sought to turn the tides by shedding light on new ideas that challenged the status quo. Modernist writers began exploring the human mind in search of true expression and freedom from the machine of government influence, producing movements like Dada and its heir, Surrealism.

Surrealism sought to create a new perspective based on a mixture of reality and dream to better explain the true expression of the human mind. Much of the inspiration behind Surrealist works can be attributed to the ideas of Sigmund Freud, a philosopher who expanded his studies into the psyche of veterans from World War I. He is responsible for the idea of the unconscious that stands as the basis for Surrealism and his ideas are clearly present in many famous Surrealist works. Franz Kafka's *The Metamorphosis* is among these works, serving as a display of many basic Freudian themes that were pertinent to the Surrealist movement. In order to understand works such as these, readers must understand their origins.

The Manifesto of Surrealism directly references Freud's ideas, as Andre Breton thanks him for contributing his partition between the conscious and unconscious. Even upon reading *The Manifesto*, the full scope of Freud's influence on the movement requires more explanation than the original document, which is often and easily quoted and misused out of context. The in-depth commentary provided by *Fifty Years Later* is effective in breaking down the dense manifesto and explaining Breton's true intentions.

Freud's Theory and *Freudian Ethics and the Idea of Reason* are both explanatory articles that lay bare the thought process and concepts that form the unconscious and conscious mind in theory. The former presents the general psychological belief while the latter puts those beliefs in context and shows how the id, ego, and superego function practically. *Beyond the Pleasure Principle* is a developmental perspective on the emergence of the three parts of the psyche, also providing evidence that Freud's concepts can be seen depicted in realistic ways, even in Surrealist works. *The Theoretical Backgrounds of Surrealism* bridges the gap between Surrealism as a movement and Freud's psychology by providing examples of the operational use of the unconscious in the production of art.

Kafka's *The Metamorphosis* is a short story that is densely packed with Freudian ideas. Throughout the story, there are examples of Surrealist beliefs that might go overlooked without a proper understanding of the psychology it is based upon. By understanding the ideas of the id, ego, and superego, readers can read more closely and understand the context and meaning of the work more deeply. This story is one of many examples that proves this point.

By aligning the ideas of Freud's psychology with a text such as Kafka's *The Metamorphosis,* the concepts he describes become clearer in the confines of the Surrealist context. Additionally, by dissecting *The Manifesto of Surrealism*, it becomes easier to pick up on how Freudian concepts might be presented through an artistic lens such as through written texts. Close readings of Freud's original ideas and the comparison to the rules of Surrealism reveal the true weight of the tripartite psyche on works from this movement.

Surrealism is a movement that began with the publication of *The Manifesto of Surrealism* by Andre Breton. Based on the idea that civilization seeks to banish any semblance of nonconforming thought or behavior, Breton claims that imagination is grossly neglected. He calls for more acknowledgment of the dreams and fantasy of individuals, as "dreams give every evidence of being continuous and show signs of organization," in contrast to reality, which humans only have some notion of with very little coordination (Breton 2). Breton sought answers about life that he believed could be found through the exploration of the unconscious (Breton 3). He coined the term "surrealism" which meant to express the true function of human thought through freeing oneself from reason and blending dream and reality (Gauss 38). Breton posits that by allowing the mind to give way to absurdity, it can relive childhood and restore the wonder previously lost and often believed to have led to the war. He focused heavily on western society and the living conditions it offered, concerned that these circumstances stifled basic human needs (Matthews 3).This obsession with the western world includes marxist beliefs about the ownership companies have over their products and employees. The demands of capitalist society seemed to stifle the Surrealist virtues of wonder, imagination, and creativity. Breton refers to the opportunity of Surrealism as "risk-free possession of oneself," a safe way to acknowledge an individual's instincts without the restraint posed by social expectations (Breton 5). He ends his manifesto with the claim that "Existence is elsewhere," as if to call to action those who seek some sort of artistic ascension from reality to something more (Breton 6).

For Surrealists, language was a medium for political and philosophical statement. According to J. H. Matthews, many believed "language employed only within reasonable bounds is language misapplied" (Matthews 4). Breton's original distinction between uses of language contrasts the "realist attitude," which confines itself to common sense and traditional logic, and the "materialist attitude," which seeks to escape the mold of utility and remove the restrictions on speech and art (Gauss 37-38). While the dislike of explicit utility is likely a marxist reflection on capitalism, the two attitudes are reminiscent of Freud's consciousness and unconsciousness too, where his idea of the tripartite mental life resides. Because of the prominence of these ideas and others in Surrealism, many authors explored further into the three parts of Freud's proposed psyche and the benefits of the conscious and unconscious.

The psychological framework of Freud's theory is composed of three parts: the id, ego, and superego. This tripartite division is largely dependent on the unconscious, with the id being majorly instinctual and without conscious reason (Rieff 169, 172). The id is ruled by bodily desires while the ego and superego mediate reason and moral function respectively (Rieff 173). Philip Rieff refers to the id as the "not self," as it is not altered by outside forces and is largely a shared set of instincts universal to most individuals (Rieff 174). The instincts in question are driven by necessity to survive, either as an individual or as a species. These include things such as eating, intercourse, and eliminating waste.

The ego functions as the judge of reason for the id, causing individuals to weigh the possible outcomes before acting on instinct (Peters 6). The development of this part of the psyche also brings about mechanisms for suppressing and coping with unfulfilled instincts. Some of these include "projection," the rejection or spitting out of things that are painful, "reaction-formation," which is essentially hoping for the best and preparing for the worst, and "isolation," the disconnecting of an idea from its emotional significance (Peters 7). Freud believed that the development of the ego fosters the Oedipus complex, which stems from an individual's desire to return to id through regression when exhausted by reason (Freud 55). The loss of energy stemming from trying to appease the ego drives the id to seek a return to simpler times, producing the final piece of the mental puzzle.

The superego is the solution to the Oedipus complex, forming as a past-choice based morality engine for easy, formulaic decision making (Peters 10). According to Freud, the superego is concerned with "the emotional factor of conviction," or morality itself (Freud 59). It is cannibalistic, absorbing the authority of parental personalities and stifling the spirit of the id even further, as it is formed out of social fear (Rieff 174, 176). The ego and superego work hand-in-hand to keep the id in check, unable to function if it were snuffed out completely. Without instinct, the other parts of the psyche have no power to express their agency. When the three fall out of equilibrium, neurosis ensues and irrational behavior reigns (Rieff 177). A healthy mind is one that has a balanced portion of each part of the tripartite psyche, each of which keeps the others reigned in, like the government's checks and balances.

In Kafka's *The Metamorphosis*, Gregor Samsa is turned into a giant vermin, forcing him to relearn to navigate the world in a new body. He experiences new challenges as he loses his job, is rejected by his family, and slowly becomes less human as a result of his transformation. One of the first Freudian concepts that is evident in the story is isolation. As Gregor finds himself waking up in an insect-like body, he disregards any concern for the state of his body, calmly choosing to focus on how it affects his morning schedule. When contemplating sleeping a bit longer, Gregor notes that he was unable, not because he was frightened, but simply because "he was used to sleeping on his right, and in his present state couldn't get into that position" (Kafka 4). His seemingly level-headedness in this situation is isolation in practice. Ultimately, Gregor isolates himself from his situation in more literal sense, running away in his final hours to die alone, the whole time disconnecting himself from reality. He wastes away alone, thinking fondly of his family despite how poorly they had treated him and agreeing that he should die as they'd hoped he would (Kafka 86). Even in this moment, he is not thinking of his approaching death, but distracting himself by rationalizing away any unsavory emotions.

Gregor also displays signs of reaction-formation on the second day of his new life as he recalls how his family had hoped to reach him the previous morning. He waits by the door in hopes that a visitor will appear to see him, but ultimately he hides, "hardly aware of what he was doing other than a slight feeling of shame," as if he expects that others will be disgusted by his presence despite yearning for the companionship of a guest (Kafka 35). Despite his desires, he is driven to act in a contradictory manner in an unconscious attempt to avoid being hurt.

The idea of projection is seen in the use of the word "hissing". Gregor recounts hissing from his father on multiple occasions, often when discussing his outbursts toward his son. In one scene, Gregor's father is said to have hissed at him three separate times, causing Gregor to call him "a wild man," despite being, himself, the one who is wild and animalistic (Kafka 29-30). Later, Gregor is said to "hiss in anger" at his sister as she yells at his mother and hisses again soon after in the presence of the three gentlemen who had taken up residence in his home (Kafka 70,78). His own hissing is first foreshadowed by the projection of such an outburst on his father, who he berates for being wild despite his own state. Based on Gregor's response to his father's actions, the reader is able to gather that he feels some sense of negativity towards his own similar behaviors.

Overall, Gregor is also a well-developed depiction of each section of the psyche as he digresses from human to creature. In the story's beginning, Gregor remains of sound mind with control of his instincts. He is shown with a healthy equilibrium, weighing options and trying to use reason to guide his choices. When he becomes aware of his predicament, he does not allow himself to be swallowed by fear or compulsion, but displays a coolness that suggests his superego has taken control and allowed him to overlook the absurdity of his situation in exchange for concern for his employer's reaction to his lateness. He becomes anxious about a visit from his boss, worried that he would be accused of laziness and convincing himself that he did "apart from excessive sleepiness… feel completely well," as if he had allowed his own self-imposed stress to manipulate his perspective (Kafka 7). His ability to rationalize and maintain his composure is indicative of a complete, well-rounded psyche that is ready and able to employ coping mechanisms where they are deemed necessary. In his desire to help those he loves, his reasoning skills, and his anxiety at the potential of a negative comment,

Gregor presents a balanced mind with id, ego, and superego intact.

As the story progresses, Gregor is forced to come to terms with his situation and accepts that he is an outcast in his home. When his family would come around to clean his space, he grew accustomed to hiding for their convenience in order to minimize discomfort. A month after his metamorphosis, Gregor "went straight to hide himself under the couch, of course," despite enough time having passed that his sister would no longer be shocked by his appearance when entering the room (Kafka 47). The phrasing suggests that, not only is this a regular practice for Gregor, but he repeats this behavior based on reasoning and consideration for the situation. He also seeks to please his sister by considering her, almost as if he is seeking a connection with her which he once had. This desire to regress becomes even clearer shortly after as he fantasizes about climbing up to "kiss her neck," which harkens back to the closeness he used to share with her (Kafka 78). Although he still has some ability to apply logic to achieve his desires, Gregor's morality drive seems to have faded, leaving him searching for a means of achieving his selfish goals, however unacceptable they might actually be. He seeks to regress back to the id, which is realistically impossible.

In the end, Gregor has regressed back to his childish beginnings with only the id to control him. He notes, in regards to his sister, "He never wanted to let her out of his room, not while he lived, anyway," as if to suggest a desire to take his her back for himself alone (Kafka 78).He is so overcome by fantasy that he's unable to escape the sight of the guests in their home. This begins his eventual downfall, which grants him one final glimpse of sanity right before his passing. His final thought was one of "emotion and love," indicating the recurrence of the ego and superego (Kafka 86). He is given a final moment of clarity right before his passing, with the brief return of his reasoning skills and morals in the end.

The Surrealist movement that was fostered by the end of The Great War gave artists and writers the ability to expand their minds to find truths about the mind from within. Vital to this movement, Sigmund Freud offered a fresh philosophical perspective on the psyche that inspired imaginative writing and creativity beyond reason. By separating the psyche into conscious and unconscious, he was able to explain how parts of the mind balance one another through a system comprised of the id, ego, and superego. Many authors explored Freudian ideas within their works, offering a psychological commentary on the state of the minds of those living in western civilizations affected by the war and the power of capitalism. One of these exploratory works is Franz Kafka's The Metamorphosis, which addresses the tripartite division of Freud's proposed psychological model and various methods of maintaining mental equilibrium through the lens of Gregor Samsa, a traveling salesman who was mysteriously transformed into an insect-like vermin overnight. In order to fully appreciate this work, readers must understand not only Surrealism as a movement, but Freudian psychology as well.

Works Cited

Breton, André. *Manifesto of Surrealism.* The University of Michigan Press, 1924.

Freud, Sigmund. *Beyond the Pleasure Principle Group Psychology: And Other Works: (1920-1922).* Translated by James Strachey, Hogarth Press : Institute of Psycho-Analysis, 1964.

Gauss, Charles E. "The theoretical backgrounds of Surrealism." *The Journal of Aesthetics and Art Criticism,* vol. 2, no. 8, 1 Sept. 1943, pp. 37-44, https://doi.org/10.1111/1540_6245.jaac2.8.0037.

Kafka, Franz. *The Metamorphosis: Franz Kafka.* Infinity Spectrum Books, 2024.

Matthews, J. H. "Fifty years later: The Manifesto of Surrealism." *Twentieth Century Literature,* vol. 21, no. 1, Feb. 1975, p. 1, https://doi.org/10.2307/440524.

Peters, R. S. "Freud's Theory." *The British Journal for the Philosophy of Science*, vol. 7, no. 25, May 1956, pp. 4–12.

Rieff, Philip. "Freudian ethics and the idea of reason." *Ethics*, vol. 67, no. 3, Part 1, Apr. 1957, pp. 169–183, https://doi.org/10.1086/291109.

The Nature of *Hamlet*: Ecology in Ophelia's Death Scene

Mae Bradley

In *Hamlet*, William Shakespeare depicts the chaos of unfolding madness through the vessel of Ophelia. The enigma of her death scene and the secretive nature of its retelling in the words of Queen Gertrude has pervaded the arts in all its forms. From the stage, it spread into literature, the fine arts, and even pop music. Each portrayal varies, but the environment in which the deceased Ophelia is found maintains the botanical essence of Shakespeare's initial presentation of her, adorned in flowers and resting peacefully in a stream. This commonality is no mistake, as the plants and environment of the scene can offer readers a deeper meaning behind Ophelia's character. By viewing Ophelia's death scene and the events leading up to it through an ecocritical lens, readers can better understand Shakespeare's intentions for her as a character in Hamlet.

Despite her function as a major plot device in *Hamlet*, Ophelia is best known for her death scene. The retelling of her passing as told by Queen Gertrude has become her identifier in many artistic formats. In the play, Shakespeare offers an image of Ophelia as a beautiful woman drowned in a river, surrounded by plants and nature. As this imagery has worked its way into the art world, artists often depict their own interpretation of the text, offering the main subject in different positions, clothes, and locations. The common thread between all of these which denotes Ophelia as the focus of the painting is environment. She is almost always in or near a river and always accompanied by a variety of botanicals.

Throughout generations of artistic interpretations of Ophelia's death, the most accurate has been an 1852 painting by Arthur Hughes, simply titled *Ophelia*. The painting itself portrays her alive and perched on a tree trunk by a river. Within the painting's lunette frame is an excerpt from Gertrude's lines in the play, which describe the specific flowers found with the body of Ophelia (Peterson 8). Other versions of Ophelia can be seen in paintings such as Eugene Delecroix's *La Mort d'Ophelie* (c, 1844). Here, the artist depicts the falling body of his subject with flowers clutched in her free arm. While the artist wished to portray Ophelia's death in progress, unlike many of his peers, he still remains true to the common identifiers of his subject (Peterson 11). In the late 19th century, various artists began adhering closely to the conventional representation of Ophelia as is well represented by Sir John Everet Millais' *Ophelia* of 1852, making her unmistakable within the flood of paintings of the time. Her standard look became that of a beautiful woman in a white dress with flowers in her hair (Peterson 12). Each of these paintings only serve as a retelling of Shakespeare's play, just as Gertrude retold the news of Ophelia's death. Their loyalty to the identifying details of Ophelia's death is proof that there is nothing that they can add to the playwright's account of the scene and emphasizes the importance of the primary text. With this in mind, it follows that the deliberate naming of flowers and herbs in the text are intentional hints toward the nature of Ophelia as a character, both in life and in death.

In studying Shakespeare, academics have often failed to separate ecocritical analyses from the simple study of nature in literature. Ecocriticism is a term that goes beyond thematic discussions of nature to a deeper meaning which commits the work to change. This study of nature includes thematic function and extends into social, historical, and theological schools of thought (Estok 110). Ecocriticism is an effective method of activism, which has popularly misled scholars to abandon self-theorizing in lieu of progressive praxis. This begs the question of whether or not ecocriticism as a movement is about nature or humanity.

A central application of ecocriticism is its use as a conduit for progress. While academics argue whether or not it is anthropocentric or not, it is undeniable that the removal of the human experience in its entirety would nullify the effects of ecocriticism on political and social levels. It is meant to push scholars in a new direction, begging for a shift in perspective that requires imagination and an understanding of complementary schools of thought (Estok 114). *In An Introduction to Shakespeare and Ecocriticism*, Simon Estok describes the gentle balance of nature and man to be founded on "ecophobia". This term is representative of a "fear of a loss of agency and control to nature," which allows for the paradigm of humans using nature as an explanatory device, and sometimes as a receptacle for blame (Estok 112). It is in this way that Ecocriticism makes the first tie between itself and Ophelia. The fear of nature is a driving force that allows its use as a scapegoat, similarly to women of the time.While in many cases, gardens began as a place of innocence and simplicity, the import of new plants and the effects of the growing world, such as new diseases and homogenization, gardens developed into an uncontrolled asset which was previously submissive to man. In this way, women who grew to be unruly or who did not submit to the male narrative were villainized and often blamed for infidelity and devious acts as they were thought of as instigators.

The idea that man has ownership over nature is parallel to man's ownership over women. While in many contexts, nature was seen as innocent and simple, this did not stop the growth of ecophobia. Over time, gardens became a symbol for status, carefully curated for the owner's tastes and fashion. Regardless of the function of gardens, they were property to be controlled and enjoyed, whether that be as a means of contemplation, science, or art (Samson 4). This level of ownership and control is reminiscent of that which men had over women during Shakespeare's time. In addition, the demand and popularity of gardens as a status symbol made room for cultural growth and a deeper understanding of political, social, and authority structures, disillusioning garden guests to the state of their surroundings. The introduction of philosophical applications of the garden experience was a first step toward the villainization of gardens. Gardens such as the "Bower of Bliss" and those that came after its destruction as a form of eulogy began to symbolize death and seduction (Samson 10). Many began to see flowering in nature as representative of sexual desire and gardeners would prune plants in order to control it, as if policing sexuality. The erotic nature of a garden was both exciting and soothing, offering the opportunity to manipulate passion deliberately with a tension between the spiritual and sensual (Samson 12). Women were also viewed as devious seductresses by nature, often thought to need the guidance of men to regulate their behaviors and thoughts. Likewise, Ophelia is used in *Hamlet* to expose the erotic economy of politics, gender roles, and family dynamics (Finklestein 18).This is depicted on many occasions in the play, such as in the first introduction to Polonius, Ophelia, and Laertes as the father states:

> And therefore must his choice be circumscribed
> Unto the voice and yielding of that body
> Whereof he is the head. Then, if he says he loves
> You,
> It fits your wisdom so far to believe it
> As he in his particular act and place
> May give his saying deed, which is no further
> Than the main voice of Denmark goes withal.
> Then weigh what loss your honor may sustain

If with too credent ear you list his songs
Or lose your heart or your chaste treasure open
To his unmastered importunity. (Shakespeare 1.3.21-31)

Here, Polonius warns his daughter not to fall for Hamlet and give up her chastity because he worries that he will use her until he is told to do otherwise and fears that his daughter does not know any better.

The ownership of gardens as a metaphor for ownership of women is evident in Hamlet and vital to Ophelia's death, caused by the shaming she suffers from her lover. Richard Finkelstein comments that Ophelia's "resistant discourse eroticizes" her opposing perspective to men, which enables the men in the play to criticize her for her sexual nature (Finklestein 14). Hamlet embodies this in his famous line "Get thee to a nunnery!", proceeding to antagonize his lover for being so available to him. He accuses her of being a "breeder of sinners", insisting she stay away from all men, as they are all "arrant knaves" (Shakespeare 3.1.119-127). The double standard of sexuality was a vessel for the vulnerability forced on women both socially and psychologically. In his emotional turmoil, Hamlet blames her for being too physically open, planting the seeds of madness in her to sprout when her father is killed. Additionally, she is, like gardens in Elizabethan England, the center of the question of ownership. Between her father and Hamlet, it is clear that there is discord about who she belonged to and which purpose she served. In the void left behind by losing the two men who had control over her thoughts and choices, Ophelia seemed to be lost in her own newly developed agency, leading her to her inevitable downfall. This was also the fate of many gardens like the "Bower" that were thought to be conduits for less than pious behaviors. The garden is also a perfect comparison for the Ophelia in its representation of death, popularized in classical Ovidian style gardens, which sought to eulogize and capture the essence of the "Bower" (Samson 10). According to Kaara Peterson, "The story of Ophelia is the story of her death" (Peterson 8). Women were seen as less than men, lacking control of meaning and thus paralleled death in their equal capacities to remove substance and significance. This is reflected in the use of "nothing" to describe female genitalia. Ophelia's beauty is a testament to the effect of doubling the evacuation of meaning, as it is a complete breakdown of significance, requiring the death of a woman to be turned into the death of a beautiful woman (Peterson18). This means that her death is meant to characterizeher,anditisher. As Gertrudestates in her reportof Ophelia's passing, she seemed to be "[Or] like a creature native and endued/ Unto that element," as if she was one with death all along (Shakespeare 4.4.78-79). As her death becomes her entire story through synecdoche, she becomes a metaphor for death, just like the garden in all its beauty.

Further evidence of the importance of botanicals in Ophelia's death lies in the scientific climate of Shakespeare's time. Horticulture emerged as a scientific field in the Early Modern period, beginning with the first major horticultural handbook, *Oeconomicus*, being published in 1508 and followed closely with more by 1526 (Samson 2). In about 1558, Thomas Hill's horticultural treatise was the first gardening handbook to be found in England (Samson 3). These handbooks became popularized as a source of information to find usefulness beyond artistic enjoyment in gardens. Over time, people began to use their newfound knowledge of botany to find medicinal uses for common plants, expanding their use into the liberal arts field instead of reserving them for mechanical arts alone (Samson 4). The popularization of horticulture affected many facets of science, but was widely used for cooking and home remedies. The accessibility of information on gardening and the use of plants, in addition to the popularity of gardening and keeping plants at the time, create relevancefor the topic in both proletarian and aristocratic lifestyles. This common ground presented a strong basis for hidden meaning in the text.

Shakespeare, himself, was no stranger to botany. Not only were herbals widely available during his time writing Hamlet, but he also grew up in an environment which afforded him horticultural knowledge prior to the popularization of herbs in his adult life. Growing up in Warwickshire offered him a rural upbringing and a deep familiarity with the uses of various plants and wildflowers in traditional medicine at the time (Dwyer 8). His own experience afforded him knowledge founded on personal experience to imbue more meaning into the flowers in the play. Following the theme of Shakespeare using his works to flex his intellect to all levels of audience, it is no surprise that he used the relevance of botanicals and florals to characterize a character as important as Ophelia.

The first use of plants as a device of characterization in the play comes before Ophelia's passing. In Act 4, scene 2, Ophelia is shown thrusting the gift of plants upon Laertes and Claudius. She tells her brother " There's rosemary: that's for remembrance. Pray you,/ love, remember. And there's pansies: that's for thoughts." Though her brother insists her behavior is a hallmark of madness, she goes on:

> There's fennel for you, and columbines.
> There's rue for you, and here's some for me; we
> may call it herb of grace o' Sundays. You must wear
> your rue with a difference. There's a daisy. I would
> give you some violets, but they withered all when
> my father died. They say he made a good end. (Shakespeare 4.2.174-179)

Fennel and Columbines are said to represent flattery and infidelity in the footnotes of the text. According to John Dwyer, columbines were also a symbol of worthlessness among Elizabethans, serving to further insult The King as a useless ruler (Dwyer6). She distributes rue to all, noting a difference in its meaning for Claudius, as it may mean grace or repentance. Her final floral mention references her father with violets, which she claims to have died off with her father (Shakespeare 4.2.170-177). Her choice of violets, associated with the death of the young, suggest that Ophelia feels a piece of herself was also lost in her father's passing in addition to the notion that he was taken from life too soon. The forward justification of her choice of herbs is both indicative of Shakespeare's intention with botanicals in his work, and the declaration of her madness brings to light the controversial nature of Ophelia's character as a woman who has autonomy. After the death of her father, she is able to think for herself but does not know how, as she's always taken orders her whole life (Smith 103). When she finally speaks her mind, Ophelia is called mad and discredited for speaking incompatibly with the male narrative, she is killed off. Even her brother, Laertes, thinks her mad, made clear in Act 4, scene 2 when he questions "O Heavens, is't possible a young maid's wits/ Should be as mortal as a poor man's life?" (Shakespeare 159-160). These claims of insanity only draw more focus to Ophelia's behavior, allowing her to serve the purpose of a "fool", revealing truths to the audience indirectly.

A major theme among the herbs and flowers listed by Ophelia is their use in medicine as emmenagogues, used to increase menstrual flow, and as abortifacients. Herbs including fennel, rosemary, rue, pansies, and violets were regularly used to regulate fertility (Dwyer 6). This deliberate choice of plants is congruent with the concept of women as a garden because of the sexual undertones. Gardens known as pleasure or walled gardens were created as a feminine space, with the garden acting as a reflection of fertility and order in the owner's household. The darker meanings behind each plant are reminiscent of the darker tones of the walled garden, which was thought to have a negative, dark and sexual property because of its shape and the maze within it. It was believed that the structure of the walled garden fostered a perfect environment for secret assassinations and secret affairs (Samson 15). This secondary meaning of the balance between fertility and abstinence was insightful for viewers who sought to understand the unspoken inner conflict Ophelia faced. Her father and lover both scorned her for her sexuality, causing confusion in their absence. Through this, her madness was portrayed to be a result of a lack of male guidance in her sex life and the allowance for agency under those conditions.

Following her offering of funeral flowers to Laertes and Claudius in the wake of her father's passing, Ophelia is not seen again, only told of in Queen Gertrude's report of her death. The importance of the flowers included in the scene of her passing is amplified by the knowledge that the report is Gertrude's retelling of a prior report of the incident. Barbara Smith's interpretation places Ophelia in a state of insanity, climbing in a tree to hang garlands of flowers and plummeting to her death (Smith 106). The text reads:

> There is a willow grows askant the brook
> That shows his hoary leaves in the glassy stream.
> Therewith fantastic garlands did she make
> Of crowflowers, nettles, daisies, and long purples,
> That liberal shepherds give a grosser name,
> But our cold maids do "dead men's fingers" call them.
> There on the pendant boughs her coronet weeds
> Clamb'ring to hang, an envious sliver broke,
> When down her weedy trophies and herself
> Fell in the weeping brook. Her clothes spread wide,
> And mermaid-like awhile they bore her up,
> Which time she chanted snatches of old lauds,
> As one incapable of her own distress
> Or like a creature native and endued
> Unto that element. But long it could not be
> Till that her garments, heavy with their drink,
> Pulled the poor wretch from her melodious lay
> To muddy death. (Shakespeare 4.4.165-182)

Regardless of intention, whether Ophelia's death was of her own will or not, it is clear that Gertrude hopes to preserve her reputation as a christian as she blames the girl's passing on the "envious silver" branch that gave way and sent her plummeting. The addition of this detail, given that she was not present for the event itself, adds strength to the assumption that The Queen might modify details of the story to suggest a narrative beyond the simple passing of Ophelia.

While Gertrude sets a full scene for The King and Laertes, she spends little time describing the general scenery of the riverbank beyond mention of the tree from which the girl fell, focusing more on listing off the garlands and flowers that accompanied Ophelia as accessories to her person. Like in Ophelia's ranting about herbs and flowers, the botanicals listed in The Queen's report hold dual meanings, allowing Shakespeare to approach the girl's character with more depth. Because of the stifling of feminine autonomy at the time, as it is expressed in *Hamlet*, the elaboration of Ophelia's character had to be executed in a subtle way. As in many of his works, Shakespeare was able to add context indirectly by using metaphor. The first of the named flowers is "Crow-Flowers", thought to represent Crow-Foots or Ragged Robins, which served as the base for garlands at the time and aligned with Gertrude's narrative that Ophelia died an accidental death while hanging ornamental flowers. The mention of Nettles and Daisies are indicative of the time period, as they were flowers which were widely distributed in England at the time (Dwyer 7). The idea of flowers used liberally for the meaningless beautification of homes and gardens is a shared trait with the way women were viewed at the time, strengthening the metaphor that women were accessories to men with little significance otherwise. The listing of three common household florals suggested that women, and therefore Ophelia, are without substance beyond their beauty.

The next flower to be found with Ophelia's corpse was said to be "Long Purples". Previously thought to represent Purple Loosestrife, another flower considered to be very beautiful, scholars now believe Shakespeare may have been referring to the Early Purple Orchid. Because of the flower's grotesque appearance, it has gained the nickname "Dogs Stones", for its tubers, which resemble testicles (Dwyer 7). The crude naming of a plant from which the scientific word for castration was born is likely deliberate, offering a commentary on the effect of male dominion over women in sexual regards. In Ophelia's case, the man who controlled her sexuality most aggressively was Hamlet. In addition, Gertrude names the "grosser named" flowers, Dead Men's Fingers (Shakespeare 4.4.170). Another member of the Orchis family, this name is believed to refer to the Spotted Orchid, which sports tubers that are divided into three finger-like lobes that resemble the swollen fingers of a corpse (Dwyer 8). It is likely that, like the flower before it, this species is mentioned to reference another man in Ophelia's life, her deceased father. The choice of two flower species of the same family was likely deliberate, each meant to symbolize one of the two men who were responsible for the madness and confusion the girl endured. By evoking the two, Shakespeare begs the question of whether or not it was the absence of male guidance or the overall control of men in Ophelia's life that caused her undoing.

The botanicals present in this passage are said to be "coronet weeds", a word describing a garland of plants. While Gertrude describes them as "weedy trophies", the meaning of the term is twofold. A coronet is also a simple crown. Suggesting that to Ophelia, these plants were more than simple garlands for hanging, but that she may also have worn them on her head, offering the audience a mental image of a would-be queen, had her princely lover not abandoned her without reason. The encircling of the crown around the head suggests the closeness of these flowers and their meanings to Ophelia's mind, which was consequently driven insane with their weight, just as Hamlet was driven mad by his own "crown", his father. Other meanings of the word deepen the meaning further, such as the use of "coronet" to describe the burr, or the base ring of a deer's antlers, which is a male-specific body part. According to the Oxford English Dictionary, the word is a borrowed word from the French which was introduced to England in the 1500s, making it relevant to Shakespeare's time ("coronet" 7). With the addition of Gertrude calling the flowers a trophy, the deer imagery is very strong. Within the male-specific mention of the burr, it is likely that there is more gender commentary present in this wording, as if to suggest the coronet is a trophy of manhood and autonomy, and the narrative that this was the cause of her falling into the river supports the idea of women being unable to survive without male guidance and dominion. What she had hunted for all along was her downfall, as was to be thought of all women.

The more obvious secondary image elicited by the use of flowers in the form of a garland is that of funerary flowers.

Garlands were and are still common tradition in funeral practice, especially as a garland or wreath to beautify and memorialize the deceased. The use of flowers in this scene and during her life are a symbol of death but also a circle, insisting upon death through the idea of a circle of life. Kaara Peterson comments that this constant state of being "dredged up' to begin her progress to death over and over" is a product of the play's needs in order to maintain stability (Peterson 18). Because the circular nature of Ophelia's timeline is necessary for the plot to maintain referential integrity, it would follow easily that Shakespeare would make the purpose of her character known in some way. This returns to the idea of women and death as the same, nothingness to the highest degree, where meaning would dissipate if not for some reason or motive.

The significance of Ophelia choosing her own funerary flowers is also important to the meaning of the text, as she again is tied to the motif of a garden as a woman. Because Ophelia is depicted as a parallel to gardens of the time, she is a vessel for the blending of poetry, politics, and nature. The planting of certain botanicals was calculated, with garden owners using choices of plants to convey a message of their choosing (Samson 5). With her father and lover gone, Ophelia was finally able to be herself. She stopped denying her own mind and "planted" the flowers that embodied her, even in her dying moments. In a way, her death perfectly represents her, not only as a beautiful woman, but as who she was and who she wanted to be. The reason that her death is so significant in her characterization is because it is the purest form of her, her deepest griefs and her inner conflict. It is not until the very end of Ophelia's life that she is truly herself because it is not until then that she may plant her own flowers in the garden that is herself. Following Ophelia's death, there is speculation about what truly happened between a gravedigger and a gentleman to whom he is speaking about her passing. They banter about the true nature of her passing and whether or not she deserves a christian burial, indicating the openness to interpretation meant for Ophelia's untimely end (Shakespeare 5.1.1-22). This indicates a desire for the audience to use the information presented to them to make their own decision on whether or not the death was a suicide, and more importantly, if she should be given a christian burial. The confusion is a product of Gertrude's retelling, which paints Ophelia in a different light than one would expect of a suicide. The conclusion of the two men in the graveyard is one that does not clarify, as they both agree the true reason for her christian burial is her status as a "gentlewoman" (Smith 107). While the men of the play do excessive amounts of talking, Ophelia is often left unable to speak for herself until her lover rejects her and her father passes along. Without their guidance and instruction, she is finally able to speak for herself, but is considered mad when her words don't suit the male narrative. The truth of Ophelia is only presented to the audience through her unbridled ramblings and the actions which are reported by The Queen following her death. Through analyzing the plants in both scenes in a literary and metaphorical context, some meaning can be derived. However, in order to receive all of the meaning intended by Shakespeare in *Hamlet* regarding Ophelia, it is important to look further to a point of ecocriticism, expanding the possibility of meaning into the social, political, and psychological. Only through deep, multifaceted understanding of the nature of Hamlet can one understand the fate of Ophelia.

Works Cited

"Coronet, n." *Oxford English Dictionary*, Oxford University press, 2024, https://www.oed.com/dictionary/coronet_n?tl=true.

Dwyer, John. "Garden Plants and Wildflowers in Hamlet." *Australian Garden History*, vol. 24, no. 2, 2012, pp. 5–34. JSTOR, https://www.jstor.org/stable/24918848. Accessed 4 Dec.2025.

Estok, Simon. "An Introduction to Shakespeare and Ecocriticism: The Special Cluster." *Interdisciplinary Studies in Literature and Environment*, vol. 12, no. 2, 2005, pp. 109–17. JSTOR, http://www.jstor.org/stable/44086432. Accessed 17 Nov. 2025.

FINKELSTEIN, RICHARD. "Differentiating 'Hamlet': Ophelia and the Problems of Subjectivity." *Renaissance and Reformation / Renaissance et Réforme*, vol. 21, no. 2, 1997, pp. 5–22. JSTOR, http://www.jstor.org/sta ble/43445106. Accessed 17 Nov. 2025.

PETERSON, KAARA. “Framing Ophelia: Representation and the Pictorial Tradition.” *Mosaic: An Interdisciplinary Critical Journal*, vol. 31, no. 3, 1998, pp. 1–24. JSTOR,http://www.jstor.org/stable/44029808. Accessed 17 Nov. 2025.

Samson, Alexander. “Introduction ‘Locus Amoenus’: Gardens and Horticulture in the Renaissance.” *Renaissance Studies*, vol. 25, no. 1, 2011, pp. 1–23. JSTOR, http://www.jstor.org/stable/24420234. Accessed 17 Nov. 2025.

Shakespeare, William. *Hamlet. The Norton Shakespeare*, vol.2, 3rd ed., edited by Stephen Greenblatt, W. W. Norton, 2016, pp. 135-223.

Smith, Barbara. “Neither Accident nor Intent: Contextualizing the Suicide of Ophelia.” *South Atlantic Review*, vol. 73, no. 2, 2008, pp. 96–112. JSTOR, http://www.jstor.org/sta ble/27784781. Accessed 17 Nov. 2025.

Plath and Salinger: Two Sides of the Same Coin

Mae Bradley

In 1963, Sylvia Plath published her iconic novel *The Bell Jar*, which centered around the maturation and mental health of a young woman named Esther Greenwood. The novel shares an uncanny similarity to J.D. Salinger's *Catcher in the Rye,* which was first printed in 1951. While both are bound to have features that parallel one another due to the nature of the bildungsroman as a genre, these coming-of-age tales are comparable on a deeper level. Underlying political themes such as fear of communism and social expectations coupled with exploration of the disturbed psyche are common between both texts, suggesting a relationship with one another. Considering these factors, it is easier to understand why many believe that The Bell Jar is inspired by Salinger's novel, calling Esther Greenwood the female version of Holden Caulfield with the added claim that they share the same political and social commentary.

The bildungsroman is a type of coming-of-age story characterized by self-discovery, feelings of isolation, and the search for a personal philosophy, often involving society and generational conflict (Wagner 55). While bildungsroman traditionally begin with a change of location, both novels are centered around New York. Holden and Esther have different personal experiences in the city, but the struggles they face are the subject of shared vices. In *The Bell Jar,* alcohol and sexual exploration land Esther in dangerous situations, such as when she is assaulted and nearly raped by Marco. Her lack of experience in drinking leads her to accept daiquiris and overdrink, ultimately landing her in a puddle of mud with her date fighting to violate her (Plath 134-139). Holden's experience with sex and alcohol also proved detrimental, as can be seen when he drunkenly summons a sex worker to his hotel room, only to be beaten for underpaying her after denying intercourse. After barhopping, Holden calls Sunny, a prostitute, up to his room and frustrates her by denying sex. She later brings her employer named Maurice to collect on unpaid charges for her time, and Holden finds himself beaten to a pulp to the point of fantasy as a coping mechanism. This is a notable example of Holden's psychosis as he would sooner choose to believe Maurice shot him than to accept that he had made a mistake that caused him to be beaten (Salinger 90-104). Salinger also offers a perspective on the dangers of deviant sex and alcohol use with the visit to Mr. Antollini's house. During a vulnerable visit with a trusted former teacher, Holden is drugged by his drunken mentor and narrowly avoids what is implied to be a molestation attempt when he suddenly succumbs to unexpected sleep and wakes to the adult man stroking his hair. He narrowly escapes by making excuses to visit his family, denying the offer to stay over and over. In hindsight, Holden notes that he thinks maybe he should have just stayed with Antolini, suggesting that he was still influenced by the substance he had been tricked into consuming and was still susceptible to being taken advantage of (Salinger 189-191). Despite the different outcomes and circumstances of the two characters' interactions with these vices, each shares a level of disenchantment and ambivalence for them. Each is interested in the idea of a hedonistic life, but finds it unfulfilling in practice, realizing that pursuing the sins often leads to danger and regret.

Another similarity between the two stories lies in the context of the politics of the time. Both stories are a testimony of life during the cold war era and are telling of the everyday pressures of the red scare and the war on communism. Plath does address the political climate more directly by beginning her story with the report of the coming execution of the Rosenbergs, but signs of societal stress and fear of otherness are present in both novels (Plath 6). In *The Bell Jar*, Esther expresses her fear and discontent with the upcoming execution, with the entire novel then following her obsession with how she is perceived and whether or not she fits in. The explicit contextualization of active McCarthyism helps in establishing concrete historical significance in the story, helping the reader to recognize the pressure individuals are under to adhere to norms within the novel (Alvarez 44). Esther seems to constantly compare herself to other women and weighs the possibilities of her future, seeking the balance between achieving her personal goals and flying under the radar. With this comes a hyper-critical lens through which Esther sees the world, which is evident when she talks about Doreen's image as a woman and even into the near-end of the novel when she finds that Joan is a lesbian (Plath 19, 280). When Esther talks about Doreen, she expresses her displeasure with how well Doreen fits in through critical remarks that cast her in a negative light, as can be seen when she claims she "knew perfectly well he'd come for Doreen," at the first meeting with Lenny Shepherd (Plath 14). Later in the evening Esther decides she no longer wants to maintain a real friendship with Doreen because she felt more kindred to "Betsy and her innocent friends," rebuking her former friend's lifestyle that she failed to thrive in (Plath 32). Even at the end of the novel, Esther suddenly cannot stand Joan after discovering her in an intimate moment with DeeDee. She comments that Joan's voice made her want to vomit and that she got a creepy feeling from her. A part of Esther's discontent reflects the sentiment of McCarthyism in rejection of otherness as she admits she simply "could never really imagine what they would be actually doing" (Plath 280). She even recalls a scandal in her college involving two women, referring to the person who discovered the scene in question as a "spy" (Plath 281). Esther has an automatic response of repulsion in encounters with women who are outside of the normal expectation for her time period, worried that affiliation with them will also turn her into an abnormality. This duality is effective in giving both Esther's conscious opinion on the state of society and showing the reader how she is at the mercy of politics on a subconscious level. Examples of this shared anxiety in *Catcher in the Rye* are subtler and come in a different form. Holden serves as a critic of social rules and a victim of them. He tends to speak in terms of specific rules, generalizations, and examples that might produce the standards which he is a slave to. Holden even justifies his unusual behaviors by applying rules to them that govern society as a whole (Nadel 351-352). One of the clearer examples of this is when Holden asks the cab driver where the ducks go when the lake in the park freezes over. As soon as the driver becomes agitated with him, Holden backpedals to justify his question, claiming "I was just interested, that's all," (Salinger 60). In trying to justify his unusual question, he creates a rhetorical purpose for his behavior, which allows it to fit in with the social norms of conversation. He also uses generalizations to pass judgement on his peers. As Holden recalls his time at Elkton Hills with roommate Dick Slagle. He comments that having cheap suitcases is enough to make him hate someone, and attempts to socially martyr himself by explaining that he would hide his own very nice suitcases to spare Dick's feelings. When describing his own suitcases, Holden states that they were "genuine cow hide and all that crap," suggesting that he really thought the suitcases were ridiculous and only used Dick as an excuse to hide them (Salinger 108). His delivery of generalizations and descriptions of things that he blatantly acknowledges to be up to social standard suggests that he is not fully subscribed to the ideals of the era, but shares

Esther's submission to the unconscious hold of society on expectation.

Both Holden and Esther are troubled by education. Esther spends most of her time back home wondering how she can get into education programs that cater to the career she truly wants. Plagued by the possibilities of the future and fearful they were unreachable, Esther spirals. Upon her first week back from New York, she weighs the options of writing her thesis, learning shorthand to appease her mother, and taking time off from school (Plath 156). Eventually, she is paralyzed by the number of options before her and fails to decide. Esther spirals as a result and finds herself in Doctor Gordon's office seeking psychological help (Plath 162). The variety of options presented to her in contrast to the difficulty of executing a plan to achieve her goals proves a long-term detriment to Esther's mental health and stunts her growth in her academic career. Plath uses the imagery of a fig tree to create a concrete depiction of the pressures of choice, which is a major factor in her eventual psychic collapse and schizophrenic symptoms (Séllei 128). In Holden's case, school is something to run from, not because he is uncertain, but because he is bored by the education system. He seems to perform well in school when he tries, but he is completely uninterested in further education. On various occasions, Holden says he wants to be a farmer or live in a cabin in the woods, but when asked what he truly wants, he says he wants to be "the catcher in the rye," preserving the youth of naive children (Salinger 173). Holden's rejection of private schools is a testament to the culture and cultivation of norms in the education system. In the end, he admits that you can't simply catch children, they have to be able to reach for the golden ring and learn from failure, a lesson learned through numerous former teachers who impose advice on Holden throughout his narrative (Nadel 368). The advice that smothers him and deters him from pursuing education comes in the form of pressure applied by Mr. Spencer and Mr. Antolini, both of whom insist he is wasting his potential (Salinger 12,182). The experiences of both characters differ based on gender, but the takeaway is the same: whether education is unattainable or expected, it adds pressure to both protagonists that drive them to rebel and ultimately succumb to poor mental health at the hands of an education system that imposes the ideals of a society plagued by McCarthyism.

In addition to common plot points, each of the novels put a focus on mental health, depicting both protagonists as mental institution patients at some point in the book, advocating for the benefits of therapy and healthcare. In *The Bell Jar,* Plath offers a glimpse into both well-done and poorly executed mental healthcare by presenting the reader with two sanatorium experiences. Although Esther is frightened and made worse in visiting the first mental hospital under the care of Doctor Gordon, she is made better under the careful care of Doctor Nolan. Plath offers her readers accounts of the benefits of treatments such as shock therapy and insulin therapy, showing that when done right, healthcare can improve the human psyche and raise an individual's quality of life. After the traumatic failed shock therapy that left Esther "wondering what terrible thing it was that [she] had done," riddled with paranoia and hallucinations, she begs to be sent elsewhere. She is carefully rehabilitated by Doctor Nolan, who makes it clear to her that the blue flashes and electrical sounds she experienced during previous sessions of shock therapy were a sign of malpractice (Plath 183, 243). Under the new doctor's care, Esther experiences a breakthrough with the help of insulin therapy, offering her some relief and helping push her toward recovery (Plath 258). When Doctor Nolan does prescribe shock therapy to Esther, she is gentle and reassuring, careful to maintain her patient's trust and triggering a pivotal breakthrough in treatment (Plath 272). Holden's stay at the mental hospital comes at the end of his novel. While he doesn't go into detail about his treatment, he does briefly admit that his hospital visit involved a psychoanalyst. Holden then goes on to admit he misses all these people he spent the novel griping about, which suggests he finally came to terms with his stress that stemmed from the nature of time and how everything is fleeting (Salinger 213-214). The pressure of decision that seemed to plague Holden is released by his therapy, which becomes apparent as he speaks about the psychoanalyst who asks him if he is planning to apply himself upon his return to school (Salinger 213). In his revelation, Holden seems to find that the pressure to decide doesn't come from what to choose, but the fleeting nature of life and its conditions (Wiegand 7). He is able to release the build up of innate need to maximize every aspect of his life and rejoin society as a child with an understanding that he is allowed to fail and grow from those unsatisfactory experiences. Although Holden doesn't claim to have received any forms of extreme therapy or treatment like Esther, his story highlights the benefit of seeking out help for individuals experiencing psychosis.

In Sylvia Plath's *The Bell Jar* and J.D. Salinger's *Catcher in the Rye,* the protagonists each represent similar values under lenses that reflect gender stereotypes and the expectations of society based on factors such as age, presentation, and the concept of McCarthyism. Beyond sharing the same general characteristics of the bildungsroman genre, the two novels share other similarities that are unique to the two. Location, time period, and political issues further tie together the two stories written within the same decade. Themes of experimentation with vices such as sex and alcohol, the red scare and communism, the pressure to succeed in academic settings, and mental health present the reader with a pair of stories that create a parallel between gendered experiences that ultimately draw the same conclusions. It is because of the resemblance between the plots of both narratives and the correlating subject matter of each that many call Esther Greenwood the female variation of Holden Caulfield with the assertion that both characters are a conduit for the same commentary on social and political conditions during the era of Plath and Salinger.

Works Cited

Álvarez, María Laura Arce. "Revisiting Sylvia Plath's The Bell Jar as a feminist response to McCarthyism." *Alicante Journal of English Studies*, no. 40, 2024, pp. 43–62.

Nadel, Alan. "RHETORIC, SANITY, AND THE COLD WAR: THE SIGNIFICANCE OF HOLDEN CAULFIELD'S TESTIMONY." *The Centennial Review*, vol. 32, no. 4, 1988, pp. 351–71. *JSTOR*, http://www.jstor.org/stable/23739261. Accessed 14 July 2025.

Plath, Sylvia. *The Bell Jar*. Faber & Faber, 2005.

Salinger, J. D. The Catcher in the Rye. Little, Brown and Company, 1991. Séllei, Nóra. "THE FIG TREE AND THE BLACK PATENT LEATHER SHOES: THE BODY AND ITS REPRESENTATION IN SYLVIA PLATH'S 'THE BELL JAR.'" *Hungarian Journal of English and American Studies* (HJEAS), vol. 9, no. 2, 2003, pp. 127–54. JSTOR, http://www.jstor.org/stable/41274242. Accessed 13 July 2025.

Wiegand, William. "J. D. Salinger: Seventy-Eight Bananas." *Chicago Review*, vol. 11, no. 4, 1958, pp. 3–19. *JSTOR*, https://doi.org/10.2307/25293391. Accessed 13 July 2025.

Wagner, Linda W. "Plath's *The Bell Jar* as a Female Bildungsroman." *Women's Studies*, vol. 12, 1986, pp. 55–68.

Unpacking The Justice System's Neglect Towards Black Women

Anaya Simon

In the United States, about 22% of Black women have experienced rape, and they are killed at a higher rate than any other racial group. In many cases, Black women and girls are blamed for the assault done to them because they are seen as "fast." This victim-blaming is powerfully showcased in the R. Kelly documentary "Surviving R. Kelly" and further illuminated in Tiffany D. Jackson's novels, "Grown" and "Mondays Not Coming." Both the books and the docuseries highlight how the criminal justice system fails to protect Black women from sexual violence due to a combination of deep systemic racism, pervasive bias against Black women, and a failure to address the distinctive challenges Black women navigate.

The six-part docuseries known as "Surviving r Kelly", is said to "describes decades of emotional, physical, and sexual abuse he allegedly perpetrated against Black girls and women" (Finoh & Sankofa, 2022). The show features more than 50 interviews which unpacks R. Kelly's twenty-year history of sexually abusing women, mostly young black girls, by using his money and fame. Kelly or an associate of his would seek out young aspiring singers, making false promises of success & a career, or even love & a family. After he recruits the victims he isolates them from their friends and families, by having the girls live with him or in one of his houses where he can monitor their movements. One of Kelly's victims, Jerhonda Pace, testified that he confiscated her cellphone, while another, named Jane, testified that Kelly discouraged all the women to speak to their friends and families because "they meant nothing" to them. (Polaris, 2021) Kelly created a supervised-supervisor relationship by manipulating his victims and keeping a strict set of rules to follow throughout their stay at whatever house he placed them at. A former assistant of Kelly testified that his victims had to ask permission to do basic things like have food or even leave room to go use the bathroom (Polaris, 2021). While the docuseries "Creating 'Surviving R. Kelly': Why dream Hampton Put Together the Powerful Series" keeps R. Kelly's criminal history of sexual abuse as the focus, the factors that have displayed a culture where black female victims of sexual abuse are ignored is not overlooked (Hubbard, 2019).

At least one in five black women are survivors of rape, and for every one in five there are at least fifteen black women who do not report the assault due to the fear of retaliation from their perpetrator (Finoh & Sankofa, 2022). They find it pointless since majority black women who do report cases of sexual assault are dismissed and at times preyed upon by those in power as well. "Black Women and Black Lives Matter: Fighting Police Misconduct in Domestic Violence and Sexual Assault Cases" states that, "researchers documented how stereotyping of sexual assault victims – a significant percentage of whom were African-American – led to poor criminal investigations and failure by police to submit thousands of sexual assault kits for testing" (Park, 2015).

Black girls are often failed by the justice system due to a process called adultification. The article "Girlhood interrupted" explains that there are 2 processes of adultification:

> A process of socialization, in which children function at a more mature developmental stage because of situational context and necessity, especially in low resource community environments and, A social or cultural stereotype that is based on how adults perceive children "in the absence of knowledge of children's behavior and verbalizations This latter form of adultification, which is based in part of adultification, which is based in part on race, is the subject of this report.
> (EPSTEIN et al)

According to a report written by Georgetown Law Center, black girls are seen as more grown-up and less innocent than their white peers, which makes others perceive them as independent. In the classroom black girls are the main target because, "[T]hey think they are adults too, and they try to act like they should have control sometimes." (EPSTEIN et al.) The quote was made by a teacher. Similarly, Tiffany D. Jackson's novels Mondays Not Coming and Grown powerfully illustrate the devastating effects of adultification. In Mondays Not Coming, the search for a missing Black teenager is complicated by how adults perceive her as independent and less vulnerable, delaying crucial intervention. Grown further explores how a young Black girl, accused of a crime, is stripped of her innocence and treated as an adult in the legal system, reflecting the biases you've already discussed.

Tiffany D. Jackson's novel "Grown" sharply illustrates the same challenges faced by Black girls that have been echoed in both real-life cases and other works discussed. The story centers on Enchanted Jones, a talented young Black girl whose dreams of stardom are manipulated by Korey Fields, a powerful music producer. Much like the survivors in "Surviving R. Kelly," Enchanted is groomed through flattery and gifts. Korey uses phrases such as "You're different" and "I see your potential" to make her feel uniquely valued, a tactic that draws her in emotionally and sets the stage for further control. This manipulative behavior quickly escalates; Korey isolates Enchanted from her loved ones, confiscates her phone, and subjects her to both psychological and physical abuse. The novel powerfully exposes how adults and the legal system repeatedly fail to intervene, blinded by systemic biases and harmful stereotypes that paint Black girls as more mature and less in need of protection. Jackson's depiction of Enchanted's journey resonates deeply with the real-world examples of adultification and neglect previously discussed, reinforcing how dangerous it is when society refuses to see Black girls as victims deserving of empathy and safety. By weaving Enchanted's story into the broader narrative, "Grown" makes clear that these are not isolated incidents—they are part of a larger, troubling pattern that demands urgent attention and change. This devastating societal indifference, rooted in the adultification of Black girls, is further compounded when their physical safety is at risk, as profoundly explored in Jackson's equally poignant novel, "Mondays Not Coming."

Tiffany D. Jackson's novel Mondays Not Coming presents a compelling narrative set in Washington, D.C., focusing on Claudia's determined search for her best friend, Monday, following her mysterious disappearance. The book's non-linear structure, featuring chapters titled "The Before," "The After," and "One Year Before the Before," effectively illustrates Claudia's escalating confusion and frustration as she endeavors to reconstruct the events surrounding Monday's vanishing. Upon returning from summer break, Claudia notes Monday's absence, which is compounded by a lack of communication throughout the summer and Monday's failure to attend the first week of school. Recognizing the gravity of the situation, Claudia attempts to alert various adults in her life; however, her concerns are consistently minimized and dismissed. This dismissal is reflected in Claudia's opening reflection: "This is the story of how my best friend disappeared. How nobody noticed she was gone except me. And how nobody cared until they found her... one year later." The consistent indifference displayed by adults in Mondays Not Coming powerfully reflects the broader systemic neglect faced by Black girls, a key argument explored through real-world cases. As the narrative progresses, Claudia's frustration intensifies, driven by the disbelief and apathy that greet her efforts to locate Monday. Monday is swiftly labeled a "runaway," and her prolonged absence is consequently trivialized, echoing the damaging effects of adultification and victim-blaming previously discussed. The novel then exposes how societal structures and their institutions frequently fail to prioritize the safety and well-being of Black girls, therefore pushing harmful stereotypes that make their vulnerabilities invisible. Jackson's portrayal of Claudia's relentless pursuit and Monday's sudden disappearance serves as a potent literary parallel to the failures of the justice system highlighted in the "Surviving R. Kelly" documentary and the novel Grown. In both the fictional novels and the docuseries, Black girls are frequently denied the essential empathy and timely intervention they require. Mondays Not Coming functions as a critical examination of these systemic failures, urging readers to recognize the urgent need for structural change. By intertwining Claudia's personal struggle with the pervasive societal issues of adultification, neglect, and systemic bias, Jackson powerfully demonstrates the critical imperative to dismantle these patterns and advocate for the protection and recognition of Black girls. The novel's opening sentence in one of the first chapters, "How nobody noticed she was gone except me" proves that societal silence and institutional indifference are not mere oversights, but active contributors to the continued vulnerability of Black girls.

Black women are consistently subjected to racial discrimination, deeply rooted in historical stereotypes that continue to shape societal perceptions. The victims of R. Kelly, along with the narratives presented in Tiffany D. Jackson's novels Grown and Mondays Not Coming, exemplify how Black women and girls are historically and presently subjected to sexual trafficking, abuses of power, and the harmful caricatures imposed by a society that systemically oppresses Black Americans. This pervasive issue, fueled by the adultification of Black girls, has been allowed to persist for generations, normalizing the neglect of Black women and perpetuating male abusive behaviors. If society is to truly reshape its views towards Black women, it is crucial to dismantle the stereotype that they do not need to be protected. Unless we fundamentally change how institutions and individuals perceive and treat Black girls, the tragic patterns of exploitation and invisibility, so vividly brought to light by R. Kelly's victims and through the fictional realities of Enchanted and Claudia, will continue to unfold.

Work Cited

"Trafficking in the R. Kelly Case: Stripping Away the Glamour to Understand the Crime." *Polaris*, 28 Sept. 2021, polaris project.org/blog/2021/09/understanding-trafficking-in the-r-kelly-case-stripping-away-the-glamour-to-understand-the-crime/. Accessed 2 Oct. 2025.

Epstein, Rebecca, et al. "Girlhood Interrupted: The Erasure of Black Girls' Childhood." *Georgetown Law,* 14 Aug. 2017, www.law.georgetown.edu/poverty-inequality-center/wp-content/uploads/sites/14/2017/08/girlhood-interrupted.pdf. Accessed 2 Oct. 2025.

Finoh, Maya, and Jasmine Sankofa. "The Legal System Has Failed Black Girls, Women, and Non-Binary Survivors of Violence." *ACLU*, 28 Jan. 2019, www.aclu.org/news/racial-justice/legal-system-has-failed-black-girls-women-and-non. Accessed 1 Oct. 2025.

Hubbard, Shanita. "Creating "Surviving R. Kelly": Why Dream Hampton Put Together the Powerful Series." *Pitchfork*, 7 Jan. 2019, pitchfork.com/thepitch/surviving-r-kelly-dream-hampton-interview/. Accessed 1 Oct. 2025.

Jackson, Tiffany D. *Grown*. Katherine Tegen Books, 2020.

Jackson, Tiffany D. *Monday's Not Coming*. Katherine Tegen Books, An Imprint Of Harpercollinspublishers, 2019.

Park, Sandra. "Black Women and Black Lives Matter: Fighting Police Misconduct in Domestic Violence and Sexual Assault Cases." *ACLU*, 7 Aug. 2015, www.aclu.org/news/womens-rights/black-women-and-black-lives-matter-fighting-police. Accessed 3 Oct. 2025.

Weida, Kaz. "Black Feminism." *Britannica*, www.britannica.com/topic/Black-feminism. Accessed 2 Oct. 2025.

Ending Deforestation in High-Biodiversity Habitats

Kasey Kuch

Imagine walking through a rainforest filled with singing birds and vibrant, green life, only to find concrete infrastructure in its place a few years later. These diverse and beautiful habitats, which you view through documentaries on your device or visit on vacation, are steadily disappearing. The consequences of deforestation for commercial purposes are wreaking havoc upon ecosystems, wildlife, causing habitat fragmentation, and facilitating the ravaging effects of global warming. "In United States from 2001 to 2024, 8.0% of tree cover loss occurred in areas where the dominant drivers of loss resulted in deforestation" demonstrates the severity of deforestation in a place that millions of people call home (Global Forest Watch). Therefore, we should strive to constrain deforestation in biodiverse habitats because it destroys wildlife ecosystems, accelerates climate change, and threatens global biodiversity.

For example, much of the human population here on Earth has somewhat contributed to the climbing rates of global warming and climate change. The everyday household items that we unknowingly use and throw away, ending up in towering landfills, are what spurs on the catastrophic outputs of global warming on Earth, Specifically, the paper that we use for school, documentation, office jobs, utensils, and for recreational purposes, such as drawing and art create such a grave outcome. Billions of trees are cut down, and countless forests are reduced to mere plots of dirt and rubble per year to meet the quota and demand for paper products all over the globe.

According to IFAW, deforestation is defined as the process of clearing and diminishing forests for the purpose of creating more available land. This newly available land can be used for agriculture, building new infrastructure, urban development, and raising livestock (International Fund for Animal Welfare). This long-standing practice occurs mainly in the South American rainforests, parts of Africa, and Southeast Asian countries such as Indonesia and the Philippines (Debanjan). This quote from National Geographic, "In North America, about half of the forests in the eastern part of the continent were cut down from the 1600s to the 1870s for timber and agriculture," demonstrates the severity of destructive economic logging in the places we live in (National Geographic Society). These areas are home to some of the richest and biodiverse ecosystems in the world. And deforestation is destroying the homes of many organisms, plants, and animals. The cutting down of trees releases increased amounts of carbon dioxide into the atmosphere (Nerger). This practice disrupts the cycle of life for many species and even indigenous human communities that depend on these habitats for resources and survival.

To expand, indigenous communities rely heavily on the valuable resources that their home and environment offer to survive. With the increase of deforestation in more recent years, many indigenous communities have been faced with the obstacles of displacement, injustice, health risks, and loss of cultural identity. According to Alokya Kanungo's "The Silent Cry of the Forest: How Deforestation Impacts Indigenous Communities", indigenous peoples have faced violent threats against their natural rights of living in protected regions of land (Kanungo). Most regretfully, many generations of these native communities are steadily losing their tradition and sacred ways of life as their spiritual and holy places are cut down and destroyed (Kanungo). The quote, "UNESCO has deemed the Sápara nation of Ecuador an 'Intangible Cultural Heritage of Humanity', due to the fact that their language and culture are in danger of disappearing," portrays how protecting these indigenous peoples' lands are crucial to maintaining sacred, historical, and ancestral culture that would be otherwise be lost (Nature & Culture International).

Additionally, the forests and environments these people live in were able to protect them from disease and ailments from the outside world, but with the unethical disregard of inhabited indigenous lands, deforestation opens native communities to harmful and even fatal diseases. This was established by "A straightforward linear calculation suggests that, on average, deforestation explains at least 22% of all COVID-19 cases confirmed in indigenous people until 31 August 2020". (Ellison et al. 40), which portrays how deforestation in indigenous communities opens their barrier to the outside world, allowing foreign pathogens to devastate whole societies of once isolated and thriving peoples. This situation has occurred time and time again throughout history, such as when Christopher Columbus and his fleets first arrived in the North American continent. The Native American people soon fell ill with smallpox, influenza, measles, and other diseases after interacting with the Europeans, wiping out millions of the Native American population.

Admittedly, some may argue that the practice of deforestation can bring economic value and social benefits when done in an organized and considerate manner. This practice provides economic benefits locally in small agrarian communities and on a global scale (Pattanayak). The practice of deforestation offers more opportunities for housing, employment, and expanding human demographics in many areas (Climate Transform). The processes of logging and deforestation provide housing and employment opportunities on the land that is used for building apartments, hotels, and corporate companies. As seen in "deforestation pros are largely economic. Logging activities around the world create jobs for those involved. They also lead to employment for those who use the cleared land afterwards," the benefits of deforestation largely support those who are in favor of the process for their personal economic gain. Supporters argue that with proper management and careful practices, deforestation can balance protecting biodiverse habitats, human processes of population disbursement, and overall growth in the economic status of many regions (Climate Transform).

However, this practice only leads to "small immediate income gain from clearing more forest", which is why it is substantial to consider the long-term and indirect effects of deforestation (Pattanayak). It seems enriching and fulfilling with the idea of the immediate gain in income through increased farming land, but as this process continues throughout decades, the innumerable acres of land utilized for agriculture will eventually become fruitless, and wildlife will steadily disappear as global warming and habitat loss progress due to the cutting down of forests and the destruction of ecosystems. One of the processes that harbors countless setbacks is the slash-and-burn agriculture technique. Shown in, "With this agricultural method, farmers burn large swaths of forest, allowing the ash to fertilize the land for crops. The land is only fertile for a few years, however, after which the farmers move on to repeat the process elsewhere," opportunities for new growth and plant life are diminished each time this invasive technique is utilized in the farming industry (National Geographic Society).

To elaborate, deforestation gradually breaks habitats into smaller, isolated areas where animals can no longer thrive in the ecosystem, forcing them to find a more suitable environment to relocate to. This process is also known as habitat fragmentation, which occurs when a habitat is broken into many small areas that are no longer connected (International Fund for Animal Welfare). The quote, “In 2023, US scientists declared 21 species officially extinct, including mammals, birds, mussels, and fish, with destroyed habitats identified as a key factor, “ establishes how the demand for more agricultural land and commercial production facilitates deforestation in areas where many generations of species of animals have inhabited for years (Simms). With the loss of shelter, food, and water, animals must find another suitable home, which can be scarce to find, reducing these once rich and lively lands to bare fields and factories.

To expand, the uprooting of trees, land, and rich soil has caused global warming rates to skyrocket. The quote, “In 2011, farms were responsible for about 13 percent of total global emissions,” displays how the purpose of creating more available farming land facilitates the effects of harmful greenhouse gases, allowing climate change to advance so far as today (Nerger). According to IFAW’s “What is deforestation and how does it impact wildlife?”, “Forests act as carbon sinks absorbing carbon dioxide (CO2) from the atmosphere and storing it in their biomass”, and when countless trees are uprooted, carbon dioxide is released into the atmosphere, “trapping heat and increasing global temperature” (International Fund for Animal Welfare).

The constant release of these harmful gases continues to deplete the protective ozone layer. These greenhouse gases include carbon dioxide, methane, nitrous oxide, and fluorinated gases (United States Environmental Protection Agency). The increase in the destruction of forests for the purpose of enriching agricultural practices is facilitating the booming rates of global warming, a largely negative impact upon every living creature on Earth. Although you may not be affected by climate change for the rest of your life, future generations of your offspring and precious animal species will face the consequences of their predecessors and suffer from what we weren’t able to constrain.

Furthermore, the demand for urban centers and the increase in deforestation is rapidly pushing many animal species towards endangerment and even extinction, creating issues of diversity in habitats. “Animal species threatened by forest loss may also face increased competition with others and can be at higher risk of being killed by predators who have also lost their natural habitat” (STAND FOR TREES). Deforestation limits resources that many animals need; competition among different species in these scarce habitats begins to surge dramatically. Due to competition for resources and habitat loss caused by deforestation, the population of weaker species begins to dwindle.

Fragmentation in habitats due to logging and deforestation also limits biodiversity due to animals being unable to find a mate, causing inbreeding, which makes a species more vulnerable to extinction, therefore causing a decrease in a species' population (International Fund for Animal Welfare). Deforestation destroys biodiversity in many environments throughout the world, which can be seen in species such as pygmy elephants, Sumatran rhinoceros, koalas, pygmy sloths, and giant pandas that are grievously affected by the loss of their habitats, since many of them do not possess the ability to help themselves out of the dire situation (STAND FOR TREES). If no action is taken, many unique and beautiful species you know of will become mere legends to future generations.

Ultimately, deforestation of prospering environments destroys the populations of animal species, creates surges in global emissions, and demolishes organized, balanced ecosystems that allow life to coexist harmoniously in these habitats. Deforestation goes far beyond harming trees; it affects the climate, wildlife, and even the people who rely on the land to survive. No matter how significant the role is, you have a part to play in protecting these crucial habitats. Together, our decisions determine the fate of whether our planet can retain its thriving glory in nature or become the barren wastelands depicted in dystopian films. To combat the encompassing effects that deforestation harbors, we can start by recognizing indigenous lands, prioritizing the conservation of natural resources, and designating territories for national parks (STAND FOR TREES). Without meaningful action, the unimaginable will become reality, but with individual and cooperative efforts, we can conserve the natural wonders of the Earth for many generations to come.

Works Cited

Climate Transform. "Deforestation Pros | What Are the Advantages of Cutting down Trees?" Climate Transform, 25 Apr. 2022, climatetransform.com/deforestation-pros/.

Debanjan. "Countries with the Highest Deforestation Rates in the World." Www.green.earth, Green.Earth, 14 Mar. 2021, www.green.earth/blog/countries-highest-deforestation-rates. Accessed 23 Nov. 2025.

Ellison, Glenn, et al. "COVID ECONOMICS VETTED and REAL-TIME PAPERS HERD IMMUNITY COULD BE EASY to REACH." CEPR PRESS, 23 Oct. 2020.
Global Forest Watch. "United States Deforestation Rates & Statistics | GFW." Www.globalforestwatch.org, Global Forest Watch, 2023, www.globalforestwatch.org/dashboards/country/USA/. Accessed 23 Nov. 2025.

Nature and Culture International. "Indigenous & Local Partners." Nature and Culture International " Bringing People Together to Save Wild Places, Nature and Culture International, 28 Nov. 2023, www.natureanculture.org/indigenous-local-partners/?utm_term=indigenous+peoples+day&utm_campaign=Our%2BWork%2B%2F%2BWhat%2BWe%2BDo&utm_source=adwords&utm_medium=ppc&hsa_acc=2265980610&hsa_cam=17004868248&hsa_grp=138729953271&hsa_ad=594345903052&hsa_src=g&hsa_tgt=kwd298001096533&hsa_kw=indigenous+peoples+day&hsa_mt=b&hsa_net=adwords&hsa_ver=3&gad_source=1&gad_campaignid=17004868248&gbraid=0AAAAADlRPw29TQXzzsHEr9vR0qXpViVku&gclid=CjwKCAiA_orJBhBNEiwABkdmjIE6JTYrg30zLcacMoJusmOU39Ri2DgjcsWtMvKL5cWMK4SBGFzjJBoCgzEQAvD_BwE.

IFAW. "Causes & Effects of Deforestation on Wildlife | IFAW." IFAW, IFAW, 31 July 2024, www.ifaw.org/journal/what-is-deforestation-impact-wildlife. Accessed 23 Nov. 2025.

International Fund for Animal Welfare. "How Habitat Fragmentation Affects Animals." IFAW, IFAW, 1 Apr. 2024, www.ifaw.org/journal/habitat-fragmentation-affects-animals. Accessed 23 Nov. 2025.

Kanungo, Alokya. “The Silent Cry of the Forest: How Deforestation Impacts Indigenous Communities.” Earth.org, Earth.org, 8 Aug. 2023, earth.org/the-silent-cry-of-the-forest-how-deforestation-impacts-indigenous-communities/. Accessed 23 Nov. 2025.

National Geographic Society. “Deforestation.” Education. nationalgeographic.org, National Geographic, 29 May 2025, education.nationalgeographic.org/resource/deforestation/. Accessed 23 Nov. 2025.

Nerger, Matt. “What Is the Relationship between Deforestation and Climate Change?” Rainforest Alliance, Rainforest Alliance, 12 Aug. 2018, www.rainforest-alliance.org/insights/what-is-the-relationship-between-deforestation-and-climate-change/?keyword=deforestation+emissions&gbraid=0AAAAAD11JQaUVRZAZL89hgTaBszAo1dzn&matchtype=p&network=g&device=c&creative=705900320386&gad_source=1&gad_campaignid=21473491397. Accessed 23 Nov. 2025.

Pattanayak, Subhrendu. “Scholars@Duke Publication: Converting Forests to Farms: The Economic Benefits of Clearing Forests in Agricultural Settlements in the Amazon.” Scholars.duke.edu, scholars.duke.edu, 1 Oct. 2018, scholars.duke.edu/publication/1262370. Accessed 23 Nov. 2025.

Simms, Dave. “How Habitat Loss Imperils US Wildlife.” Earth.org, Earth.org, 12 Feb. 2024, earth.org/lost-species-the-impact-of-habitat-destruction-in-the-us/. Accessed 23 Nov. 2025.

STAND FOR TREES. “Death in the Forest: Deforestation Effects on Animals and What You Can Do.” Stand for Trees, Stand For Trees, 23 Oct. 2021, standfortrees.org/blog/deforestation-effects-on-animals/. Accessed 23 Nov. 2025.

United States Environmental Protection Agency. “Overview of Greenhouse Gases.” US EPA, US EPA, 16 Jan. 2025, www.epa.gov/ghgemissions/overview-greenhouse-gases. Accessed 23 Nov. 2025.

Works, Wildlife. "Death in the Forest: Deforestation Effects on Animals and What You Can Do." Stand for Trees, Stand For Trees, 22 Oct. 2021, www.standfortrees.org/post/death-in-the-forest-deforestation-effects-on-animals-and-what-you-can-do. Accessed 23 Nov. 2025.

What Changed My Life

Kristopher Adams

A significant experience that changed my life for the worse happened on Wednesday 09, 2020. This was the day my father passed away. His passing was the hardest thing I had ever gone through, especially since I was thirteen years old. I remember it like it happened yesterday. He was not just my dad, he was my best friend, the person I could talk to about anything, and was also my biggest supporter. So, when I lost him, it felt like I had lost a piece of myself. As a child, it is a nightmare to hear that a child's father is gone and he is never coming back. The moment that I heard that my world turned upside down. This traumatic event really shaped me into the person who I am today and left a permanent mark on my life. He played a tremendous role in my life and the strength I have built.

When my dad was alive, he was the most chill and laid-back person you could have ever met. People loved talking to him because he was the kind of person you could always lean on and vent about anything, and he would not judge you. He really loved kids, and even if they weren't his he loved them all unconditionally, I think that's a big part of why he became a little league football coach. Any kid he met he treated them like were family. He was always trying to get new kids on the team even if they didn't have a ride. He would tell them to call their parents and try convincing their parents to let them play football and every time they did it. My dad even offered to pick them up and drop them off. So before the practice he would have to leave the house an extra hour early so he could round up all the kids of that were riding with him to practice getting them there. If they needed a ride to the game, he told them that they had to spend the night at his house to make sure they got to the game in the morning. He cheered for everyone, I can still hear him yelling from the sidelines saying, "Run that ball, boy, or block!" So many kids looked up to him just like I did. Watching his coach skills really showed me how much my dad really cared about kids.

For years my dad struggled with health problems for years. Growing up they told me that he had a heart attack so bad where he had to have major surgery and had to live with a pacemaker until he could get a new heart from donor. He lived with that pacemaker for nine years until one day the doctors told us he was able to get a heart transplant. I was really excited, but on the low very scared, but I knew I had to stay strong because this surgery could give him a new chance in life. But like a month after surgery, his organs did not want to accept the new heart transplant because he had the pacemaker for so long and he unfortunately passed away.

The time that I found out will never leave my mind. I was sitting at the doctor's office with my Nana when my mom called and she said "He's Gone". At that moment all I could do was look at the doctor and my Nana and burst into tears. My heart was shattered into a thousand pieces; all I could do was cry. I was devastated, numb, and all I could do was shiver. The news seriously didn't feel real; it felt like a dream I wish I could have woken up from. I could not believe what was happening, it felt like a piece of my heart was gone. I knew nothing was going to be the same without him, and one of the people I could call on was no longer there. The holidays did not feel real anymore no matter who's house I was at. It still felt something was missing because I was unable to tell him, "Happy Thanksgiving", or tell him what I got for Christmas, or that I was ready to go to his house so I could open my gifts there.

Another time that it really hit me that he was gone was when I graduated. That day was supposed to be the best day of my life, but it kind of was not because he was not there to cheer for me like he had always done and I was not able to chunk up the deuces or nod at him while I was walking up. I felt so unreal but real at the same time, I just kept wishing that he could have been there to see his first biological son graduate from high school.

After my dad passed, my life became difficult. I fell into a deep depression that lasted a long time. I was not motivated anymore, I did not want to do anything, nothing was making me happy, and the things that mattered to me at first did not matter to me anymore. Like I did not want to do online school, I did not want to play outside, and I did not even want to go the store when everyone was asking all I wanted to do was sleep. Every time I looked at my little brother, the youngest one, I would cry because he was only six years old and had to grow up with no dad. I also did not to be around people and stuff that reminded me of him. It would send me into a panic attack.

Then for years I walked around with a chip on my shoulder that caused me to argue with my mom and stepdad over the smallest things. Really, deep down, I was afraid my stepdad was going to try to take my real dad's place, and I thought my mom was going to let it happen. The fear made me push him away and argue with him even when he was right and not doing anything wrong. Honestly, I just did not know how to tell them the truth about I was truly feeling and how broken I felt inside. Instead of talking about my feelings, I just bottled it up until I exploded into anger. I honestly felt alone even though I was not. I kept on thinking they were not going to understand my pain, so I pushed them away without realizing it and I truly regret it. Losing my father did not just affect me emotionally; it changed the way I acted and looked at everything, and even the way I treated my mom and stepdad.

Even though I was hurting deeply, I had to remind myself about all the good times I had with my dad. Now when I miss him, I think about those moments a lot. I miss sitting in front of the house with him, talking about our life and future. He used to always tell me when he was not sick anymore, he was going to take me to Disneyland and teach me how to drive. I also miss going to our family reunion in the summertime seeing all of us come together having fun and just enjoying each other's company. The block party that they had the night before was always the best because we would pop fireworks, have food and games. Still his passing did change some things for the better, three out of seven of my siblings got really close to each other, and I also got close to my stepmom. My sister and I talked on the phone almost every day after he passed. We would talk about everything, and everybody would also vent, laugh, and talk about memories with our dad. We were really helping each other heal. Having them to lean on made me feel less alone because they knew my pain. Before I got older, I used to spend every weekend with my stepmom and her kids. They were a big support system at the time. Being with him during those times made me feel still connected because they stayed with him every day twenty-four seven. Even though losing my dad changed my relationship with people, I thought they would leave me. Yet it taught me that I am not alone as long as they are by my side.

After all that I had gone through losing my dad, I had really realized that I needed to change the way I communicated with my mom and stepdad. Usually, I would just hold everything in, because I did not want to show my true thoughts and feelings. But, with me keeping my emotions in it only caused me to have outbursts and be angry at them. As time went by, I started to open more and be truthful about how I felt instead of shutting them out. Our relationships got better, and I am not scared to tell them what's wrong and what I need. Learning to show my emotions and say how I really feel helped me think about my future and why I chose the career path I'm going for today.

Losing my dad was the most significant and painful experience of my life. It was something that I never imagined I would have to face at a young age. His death changed me in ways I'm still trying to understand, and the grief I carry will always be with me. I will hold on to all the love and support he gave unconditionally until I can't anymore. I will tell myself if I can go through that challenge at such a young age I can go through anything. In his memory and for myself I will always be grown and be focused and do not let anything get in the way of my future and that I am going somebody that he is proud of.

Art

Contributor Biographies

Kristopher Adams
Kristopher Adams is a college freshman who was born and raised in Houston, Texas, by Carolyn Adams and Bashuda Davis. He comes from a large family, with nine biological siblings and four step-siblings, which has shaped his strong sense of family and responsibility. Kristopher enjoys cooking and values spending quality time with his loved ones. After graduating from college, he plans to become a social worker so he can help support and guide children in need.

Jordan Albert
Jordan Albert is a photographer and an editor living in the Southeast Texas area. He creates his pieces using a digital camera and is still relatively new to the field. He would like to capture subjects through his lens and show the world a vibrance that his eyes can see. He continues to find and share the vibrance in man-made creations, structures, and nature.

Mikaela Bartlett
Mikaela Bartlett is an English major and Communications minor. She works as a reader and typesetter in the Pulse Magazine team. Some of her hobbies including reading, baking, theater, and playing with her dogs, Zola and Rafael. Mikaela has been writing all kinds of things for as long as she can remember, but poetry has always held a special place in her heart. She's grateful for this opportunity to share her poems and be a part of Pulse!

Joseph Bernard
Joseph Bernard is a student at Lamar University, who is going for a history degree. They enjoy things like writing, reading, games, and anything else that could express their creative side. They were shocked to hear that their piece was being accepted. They are currently writing something much longer, and they hope it would be much better than the short story.

Mae Bradley
Mae Bradley is a Graduate student pursuing a Master's of English at Lamar University. They have a focus on literary elements and

poetry, which translates into their contributions to the Pulse publication. Recently, Mae has also dipped into the fine arts through watercolor painting. This is their second year as Poetry Editor and a contributor for the literary magazine. When asked what inspires them to write and create, they would likely say their cat, Jericho.

Claudia Cooper
Claudia Cooper is a first-year graduate student whose interests lie in Afrofuturism and other Black diaspora studies. This is her second year as editor-in-chief and fourth year working on the Pulse team. It's her third year contributing to Pulse with this year's poetry submissions inspired by dreams and childhood memories.

Isabella Deese
Isabella has started and ended her college career with a publication to Pulse magazine. Her debut poem "Today" can be found in the 2022-2023 Pulse edition. Isabella enjoys learning new crafts, watching cat videos, and sitting outside in the sunshine. Look out for future publications from Isabella as she graduates this semester with her B.A. in English.

Oakley Eligio
Oakley Eligio is a hobbyist writer with a passion for classical literature and poetry. They take inspiration from their environment and their relationships with others as the basis for their work. Their favorite color is purple, and their favorite people are their siblings!

William Hammers
William Hammers is a Senior at Lamar University majoring in Psychology and minoring in English. After graduating, he intends on starting a master's program in Clinical And Mental Health Counseling here at Lamar. Will is an avid reader, loves to play video games and tabletop RPG's, and works out regularly.

Jonas Hatch
Jonas C. Hatch is a current Sophomore studying physics at Lamar University. Much of his work revolves around the ideas of existential nihilism, the subjective nature of reality, and of what it

means to be human. In his free time, Jonas enjoys doing art, reading comics, and playing board games and RPGs with friends.

Keith Hoffpauir
English Major, Philosophy Minor at Lamar University. A non-traditional student, Keith has traveled extensively throughout and lived in different areas of the United States. He has held many different jobs ranging from day laborer, fry cook, and industrial painters' helper to lumberjack, hotel night auditor and middle management.

Bronwyn Jones
Bronwyn Jones is a senior at Lamar University graduating in May 2026, where she studies English with a minor in Writing. Her work is drawn to the natural world and the quiet it holds. Outside of writing, she crochets and plays video games, often at the same time.

Kasey Kuch
Kasey Kuch is a Texas Academy junior at Lamar University. She is an Electrical Engineering major, and is part of the IEEE, SASE, and LU Book Birds student organizations. She is also part of the Social Media committee of Texas Academy and is junior representative of the RED Robotics club of Texas Academy and the College of Engineering. Kasey finds enjoyment in reading, writing, playing tennis and pickleball, and spending meaningful time with family and friends.

Gillian Laird
Gillian Laird is a young writer from Southeast Texas who is currently getting her MA in English. She is also hard at work on her debut novel. More of her writing can be found in literary magazines such as Pulse and Outrageous Fortune, as well as the Lamar University Press and Free the People.

Alexander Lara
Having both Mexican and Guatemalan ancestry, Alexander hopes to continue to share his experience that is often overlooked. Through his parents' sacrifice, he continues to push forward. Being a First-Generation student, he had always wanted more, more

achievements, and more experience. Early on, he understood being at a place like Lamar was a privilege that must not go to waste.

Trinity Levins
Trinity Levins is a freshman English major. They enjoy reading, writing, making art and music, and going to local shows in Beaumont. They also work at KVLU Public Radio as a student producer/assistant.

Adithleidy Lopez-Magallon
Adithleidy Lopez-Magallon is a Biology major with a concentration in Pre-Medicine and a minor in Spanish. She is passionate about serving her community and often volunteers as a translator. Her experiences have inspired her to pursue a career in medicine, where she hopes to support Hispanic patients during vulnerable and critical moments.

Da'Vonna Martin
Da' Vonna Martin, 22, raised in Beaumont and is a senior studying American Sign Language. She writes heartfelt poetry to express emotions words alone can't hold, turning personal experiences into connection, healing, and understanding for both herself and others.

Jocelyn Rico
Jocelyn Rico is a current sophomore at Lamar University and studying English while pursuing her teaching certification. She is a 2024 graduate of Thorndale High School and first- generation college student. Jocelyn's writing is deeply rooted with her Hispanic culture which inspired her short story "Divided."

Yoseli González Rodríguez
Yoseli González Rodríguez is an artist in several fields. She currently dedicates most of her time to acting and writing in both professional and amateur settings, but has been drawing and illustrating for the longest. Inspired by the works of William Shakespeare, Mary Shelley, and Oscar Wilde, Yoseli illustrates depictions of literature.

Anaya Simon
Anaya Simon is a Criminal Justice student at Lamar University exploring the moral complexities of American literature, with a

focus on systemic racism and the neglect/injustice of Black women. Anaya aspires to become a defense attorney, where she hopes to push for legislative change and fix the rigidities of the current legal system.

Hailey Waobikeze

Hailey Waobikeze is a Communication-Advertising senior at Lamar University with a passion for storytelling and creative expression. She enjoys creating multiple forms of art, including writing, painting, and drawing, in order to make others feel something, and she aims to inspire through both her academic and creative work.

Jeri Wolfe

Jeri Wolfe graduated from Lamar University in 2023 with a Bachelor of Arts in English. Now in her graduate degree, she is a free-time poet who aspires to work in marketing. She finds joy in crafting poems that explore the human experience. Wolfe's poetic journey is a testament to her passion for language and highlights her goal to capture the nuances of life through words.

Teri Wolfe

Teri Wolfe is in the process of getting her master's degree in English at Lamar University. She has an interest in the arts—particularly writing, drawing, music, and theatre. While she likes to create her own works, she finds enjoyment in other people's creations and gets easily inspired from their contagious passion to create. With her degree, she plans on becoming an instructor, or a comic book illustrator and writer (whichever comes first).

Rylee Zapotoschny

Rylee Zapotoschny, contributor of "Ideals," is a Texas Academy student at Lamar as a political science major.

Pulse Staff Biographies

Mikaela Bartlett
Mikaela Bartlett is an English major and Communications minor. She works as a reader and typesetter in the Pulse Magazine team. Some of her hobbies including reading, baking, theater, and playing with her dogs, Zola and Rafael. Working as a reader and typesetter for Pulse has honed her skills in editing and has encouraged her passion for writing. She's grateful for this opportunity to be a part of Pulse!

Mae Bradley
Mae Bradley is a Graduate student pursuing a Master's of English at Lamar University. They have a focus on literary elements and poetry, which translates into their contributions to the Pulse publication. Recently, Mae has also dipped into the fine arts through watercolor painting. This is their second year as Poetry Editor and a contributor for the literary magazine. When asked what inspires them to write and create, they would likely say their cat, Jericho.

Noah Carey
Noah is an aspiring writer who focuses on Fantasy and Sci-Fi writing. From a young age, they were always invested in mythologies, space, and fantastical creatures. Now, they aspire to write many kinds of novels and capture that inspiration, all while making their own.

Brooke Graves
Brooke Groves is a freshman in her second semester. She has been in Pulse for two semesters as the poetry reader and proofreader. As an English major, she aims to be a high school level English teacher. She likes to read, write, and sleep in her free time.

Britton Larson
Britton Larson is a first-year graduate student pursuing a Master's degree in English. Not committing to any particular avenue of study, he enjoys learning about anything. Britton has been on the Pulse team since 2022 and has published poetry in two of Pulse

books. He is excited to have worked on this year's publication and looks forward to the next one.

Savanna Peveto-Kreatschman
Savanna Peveto-Kreatschman is a graduating senior majoring in English and minoring in writing. This is her second year as prose editor for Pulse. Her friends best know her for her quirky personality and ability to sidetrack classroom discussions. In her spare time, she enjoys reading, writing, crocheting, and spending time with loved ones.

Jocelyn Rico
Jocelyn Rico is a Prose Editor at Pulse Literary Magazine, currently in her first year with the publication. A sophomore at Lamar University studying English and pursuing her teaching certification. She is also a first-generation college student and graduate of Thorndale High School.

Shakarral Singleton
Shakarral Singleton is an English major and Communication minor. She has always been big on reading and learning more about literature, and she enjoys writing and the process of filmmaking. She aspires to publish her own books and teach during and after her career.

www.ingramcontent.com/pod-product-compliance
Lightning Source LLC
LaVergne TN
LVHW010903110826
845149LV00005B/1455